Johnny May's Guide to
PREVENTING IDENTITY THEFT

Johnny May's Guide to

PREVENTING IDENTITY THEFT

**How criminals steal your personal information,
how to prevent it, and what to do if you become a victim**

Johnny May's Guide to Preventing Identity Theft
Published by Security Resources Unlimited, LLC

For information on ordering and distribution, visit
www.identitytheftinfo.com or contact secres@prodigy.net

Disclaimer: The information presented in this guide is accurate to the best of our knowledge. Every effort has been made to provide the reader with a tool that is useful and accurate in combatting the crime of identity theft. The reader is solely responsible for any application of the information presented in this guide. This book was written for informational purposes only. for legal advice consult with an attorney.

Library of Congress Control Number: 2003098316

Cover and interior design by Pneuma Books, LLC   *
Visit www.pneumabooks.com for more information.

Printed in the United States
10 09 08 07 06 05 04   5 4 3 2 1

Publisher's Cataloging-in-Publication Data
(*Prepared by The Donohue Group, Inc.*)

May, Johnny R.
 Johnny May's guide to preventing identity theft : how criminals steal your personal information, how to prevent it, and what to do if you become a victim / by Johnny May.
  p. cm.
 Includes bibliographical references and index.
  ISBN: 0-9724395-0-1
1. Identification cards--United States--Forgeries. 2. False personation--United States--Prevention. 3. Swindlers and swindling--United States. 4. Commercial credit fraud--United States. 5. Fraud--United States--Prevention. 6. Credit cards--Forgeries. 7. Internet fraud. 8. Computer crimes. 9. Imposters and imposture. I. Title. II. Title: Preventing identity theft.

HV6679 .M39 2004
364.16´3--dc21   2003098316

This book is dedicated to my friends, family, and colleagues for all their moral support and patience.

Acknowledgments

Thanks to Pneuma Books, LLC, for designing my book and turning my dreams into reality.

Table of Contents

CHAPTER ONE

Identity Theft: An Overview

Identity theft has received its fair share of media attention in recent years. You've heard about it on the news. You've read about it in the paper. You've probably even seen humorous television commercials about it. But identity theft is no laughing matter.

The crime of identity theft has reached epidemic proportions. The Federal Trade Commission recently released a survey that revealed identity theft claimed a whopping 27.3 million victims over the past five years.[1] The number of inquiries received by the fraud units of consumer reporting agencies is also at an all-time high, this is due largely to increased public awareness about identity theft.[2]

The Federal Trade Commission (FTC), the leading governmental agency addressing the problem of identity theft, has reported a dramatic increase in the incidence of this crime. For example, In November 1999, the FTC Clearinghouse answered an average of 445 calls per week. By March 2001, the average number of calls answered had increased to over 2,000 per week. In December 2001, the weekly average was about 3,000 answered calls.[3] In testimony to a U.S. Senate Judiciary subcommittee, FTC Consumer Protection Bureau Director Jodie Bernstein said, "The fear of identity theft has gripped the public as few consumer issues have."[4]

Why all the fear? Most likely it's because a target of identity theft usually doesn't know he has become a victim until he has a credit application denied or receives a phone call from a collection agency seeking payment. It is a very troubling prospect!

What Is Identity Theft?

Identity theft occurs when someone uses the identifying information of another person-name, Social Security number, mother's maiden name, and so forth -to commit fraud or engage in other unlawful activities.[5] While numerous variations of the crime exist, an identity thief can fraudulently use personal identifying information to:

- open new credit card accounts;
- take over existing credit card accounts;
- apply for loans;
- rent apartments;

- establish services with utility companies;
- write fraudulent checks using another person's name and account number;
- steal and transfer money from existing bank accounts;
- file bankruptcy; and
- obtain employment using the victim's name.

Ironically, the dollar losses aren't the greatest concern for most victims. The real problem for most victims, as you'll soon find out, is straightening out a damaged credit history.

Financial Impact

Identity theft is difficult to track because it can range from a simple unauthorized use of a credit card to complete takeover of a person's identity. But no one doubts that the financial impact is substantial - and growing rapidly. According to the FTC, identity theft losses to businesses and financial institutions in 2002 totaled nearly $48 billion dollars.[6] During the same year, Mastercard and Visa officials provided the U.S. General Accounting Office with information on their fraud-related dollar loses for calendar years 1996 through 2000. For domestic operations, those losses — account takeovers and fraudulent applications — rose from $79.9 million in 1996 to $114.3 million in 2000, an increase of about 43 percent.[7] Identity theft also involves indirect costs. All of us pay when companies increase their prices to recover losses due to identity theft.

Who's at Risk

When asked about identity theft, most people say, "It will never happen to me." But some experts say it's no longer a matter of *whether* you will become a victim of identity theft, but *when*.

A common misconception is that only the wealthy or creditworthy are targeted by identity thieves. The truth is *no one is immune*. Anyone with a Social Security number is at risk. Identity theft is a crime of opportunity. Identity thieves will impersonate anyone whose information they can obtain — even if it's from an obituary!

Here is just one example. A North Dakota man received a call from his bank. The loan officer wanted to know why he had applied for a loan to buy a new pickup when he had just taken one out for a new vehicle. Then he received a call from another bank asking for payment on bounced checks totaling almost $9,000. The real shock came when he went to renew his driver's license in the same town where he grew up. The clerk looked at the man, then at the records, and told the man that he was not who he said he was. The computer spit out a license with the victim's name and another man's photo on it. The thief, a veteran con artist, had obtained a copy of the victim's birth certificate for $10 from a gullible state employee. How had the con man picked out his victim? From an obituary for the victim's deceased brother.[8]

Children have also been exploited by identity thieves. In one case, a man was arrested for allegedly stealing the identities of dozens of students at an Idaho elementary school. The man took over their identities after gaining access to the schools enrollment records.[9] It's also not uncommon for parents with derogatory credit histories to open utilities and apply for credit using their children's names.

Even the deceased are at risk. A man posing as a state's department of revenue agent used personal identifying information about recently deceased people to apply for credit cards. The man allegedly learned the identities of the recently deceased and then tricked funeral homes into providing telephone numbers of surviving spouses and contacted them, claiming he was a tax agent who needed information about their dead mates for final tax returns.[10]

Seniors should also beware. In Detroit, identity thieves located houses that were owned free and clear by elderly people. Then, they stole the owner's identity and drained the equity of those houses without the owner's knowledge or consent.[11]

Other popular targets of identity thieves are people with common names, as well as mothers, daughters, juniors, and seniors with the same name. "Identity thieves exploit the inherent confusion over such names," said David Szwak, a Louisiana attorney who has filed more than one hundred lawsuits on behalf of identity theft victims.[12]

According to the U.S. Census Bureau, here are some of the most common names in the United States:

- **Family names:** Smith, Johnson, Williams, Jones, Brown, Davis, Miller, Wilson, Moore, Taylor

- **Male names:** James, John, Robert, Michael, William, David, Richard, Charles, Joseph, Thomas

- **Female names:** Mary, Patricia, Linda, Barbara, Elizabeth, Jennifer, Maria, Susan, Margaret, Dorothy

The bottom line is that the more common your name, the more at risk you are.

Why Identity Theft Is Attractive to Criminals

Criminals are attracted to the low risk and high rewards that identity theft provides. First of all, the law treats identity theft as a crime against property, and in general the penalties for property crimes are less severe than for crimes against a person. Most career criminals know this. They also know that the majority of law enforcement attention goes to high-profile crimes, such as homicide, rape, and robbery.

Another major problem is that credit card companies are rarely willing to prosecute identity thieves. This has become an accepted business practice for the credit card industry. In most cases, the fraudulent charges are written off as the cost of doing business and passed along to consumers in the form of higher interest rates.

To make matters worse, police departments often lack the resources to properly investigate identity crimes. The thieves are seldom apprehended. Even when brought to justice, they usually receive lenient sentences. In most cases, that sentence is usually community service or probation.

Motives of the Identity Thief

Identity thieves steal for various reasons, but there are three main motives:

- **Financial gain.** This is the most common reason for identity theft. The goal is to drain all bank and credit card accounts and then move on to the next victim.

- **Revenge.** their main goal is to avenge perceived mistreatment, or to ruin the victim's credit history and reputation. This may be accomplished by creating a criminal record or derogatory credit history using the victim's name.

- **Fresh start.** By assuming someone else's identity, the identity thief can cover up a criminal record or a poor credit or employment history and lead a "normal" life. There are actually books for sale that teach how to use counterfeiting and other techniques to establish a new identity - an identity with good credit.

Victim Survey Data

The California Public Interest Group (CALPIRG) and the Privacy Rights Clearinghouse conducted a survey of sixty-six identity theft victims. The survey, which explored the specific problems encountered by victims of identity theft, revealed the following:

- The average victim learned about identity theft fourteen months after it occurred.

- More than half (55 percent) of the victims considered their cases unsolved at the time of the survey, are their cases had been open an average of forty-four months.

- Victims spent an average of 175 hours actively trying to clear their names.

- The average total fraudulent charges made on new and existing accounts was $18,000.

- Victims felt the police had been unhelpful. The survey revealed that officers issued police reports less than 75 percent of the time and assigned a detective to the case less than half the time.

- Respondents found out about identity theft in one of two ways: they were denied credit or a loan because of a negative credit report stemming from fraudulent accounts, or a creditor or debt collection agency contacted them about payment.[13]

The Identity Theft Resource Center took on the task of updating information and benchmarking it against information that had been collected over the past several years. Their study, Identity Theft: The Aftermath — 2003, details the following: economic impact of identity theft on victims and the business community, responsiveness of entities with whom the victim must interact, and the first quantification of the emotional impact of this crime on its victims.

The study found:

- Victims now spend an average of 600 hours recovering from this crime, often over a period of years. Three years ago the average was 175-200 hours of time, an increase of more than 300 percent.

- The business community loses about $92,000 per name in fraudulent charges, an increase of more than 500 percent from data in 2000.

- Victims spend an average of $1,400 in out-of-pocket expenses, an increase of 185 percent from years past.

• Approximately 85 percent of victims found out about the crime due to an adverse situation — denied credit or employment, notification by police or collection agencies, and so forth.

• Victims report a lack of responsiveness from those they turned to for help similar to the results reported in Nowhere to Turn, a survey conducted by The Privacy Rights Clearinghouse and CALPIRG in 2000.[14]

In fairness to the police, it should be noted that until 1998, there were almost no statutes making identity theft a crime or specifying police response. Also, there was little in the way of financial support for departments to deal effectively with this issue. That is changing - rapidly — and both laws and resources have been brought to bear in many states. Many police departments now have special task forces to deal with crimes of identity.

Identity Theft and the Law
The majority of states now have some form of identity theft law on the books. These laws, however, vary greatly in their form and scope as to how identity theft is defined and punished. The American Legislative Exchange Council, the nation's largest bipartisan mem-

bership organization of state legislators, has created a model bill, titled the Personal Information Security Act (see Appendix J). The model legislation draws from many of the best practices employed around the country.[15]

Meanwhile, at the federal level, Congress passed the Identity Theft and Assumption Deterrence Act of 1998. This law made it a federal crime when anyone....

...knowingly transfers or uses, without lawful authority, a means of identification of another person with the intent to commit, or to aid or abet, any unlawful activity that constitutes a violation of federal law, or that constitutes a felony under any applicable state or local law.[16]

Violations of the act are investigated by federal investigative agencies such as the U.S. Secret Service, the FBI, and the U.S. Postal Inspection Service and prosecuted by the Department of Justice.

Johnny May

CHAPTER TWO

Technology and the Information Age

The adage "Information is power" holds true in today's high-tech computer age. The computerization of personal information has created a whole new type of criminal. Records and information, which once took days or weeks to obtain, can now be gathered in a matter of minutes or hours using a home computer. Today, if a person has money and desire, there's almost nothing he or she can't find out about you.

For example, access to driver's license information has traditionally been restricted to law enforcement officials. But now some states allow the purchase of such information over the Internet. South Carolina and Florida officials sold millions of digital photos of driver's licenses to private companies. As you might expect, this raised serious questions about personal privacy.

After numerous consumer complaints, both states placed greater restrictions on the sale of digital photographs.[1] However, it is nevertheless becoming more common for consumers and companies to seek and gain access to this information.

Computers and the Internet

Computers make it possible for anyone to gather personal information about each and every one of us. Much of this information is available for a price on the Internet. In a recent case, a California woman downloaded credit reports from the same websites used by landlords to conduct background checks on prospective tenants. Some sites sent her the credit reports after nothing more than a mouse-click promise that she would use the information legally. At the time of her arrest, the woman had financial data on more than three hundred people.[2]

A curious news correspondent recently decided to see just how easy it is to get supposedly confidential financial records from such credit-checking sites. It took him only two minutes and $14.95 to access his spouse's credit report.[3]

The Internet has done two things. First, it makes public records quickly accessible to anyone who wants them. Even though most of this information has always been a matter of public record, how to access it has not been common knowledge. Now anyone with a computer and Internet access can obtain it. The second thing the

Internet has done is allow identity thieves to work anonymously from anywhere in the world. In the past, a criminal would have to visit a bank or lending institution to apply for an account, increasing the risk of being captured. With instant credit on the Internet, a criminal is highly unlikely to be captured, while the prospective reward for the thief has increased. A smart crook working on the Internet may turn a tax-free gain of as much as $50,000 per week. Compare this to the bank robber who passes a note to a teller and if he's lucky walks off with $1,000.[4]

Today, an identity thief armed with a Social Security number and other personal information can apply for credit cards over the Internet with little scrutiny from card issuers. Shopping on the Internet is also easy because the credit transactions are not made face-to-face. By using a credit card a few times and paying monthly balances, the identity thief can quickly establish what appears to be a solid credit history — and gain the credibility to apply for items with a high dollar value, such as cars.

"Hacking" is also becoming more common as a means to commit identity theft. A hacker slips by electronic security and password barriers to gain access to a company's computer server, or sometimes the server of an Internet service provider (ISP). Then they steal names, addresses, credit card numbers, and other information. In one case, individuals hacked into an ISP computer server and stole the records for 10,000 customers. Then they sent a message to the ISP offering to return the stolen data for $30,000. In the end, the hackers were apprehended and charged with extortion – but only after doing considerable damage.

Identity thieves also use phony websites to commit their crime. For example, one cyber-criminal decided to impersonate the FBI in order to obtain Social Security numbers and other personal information. He put together a fake website complete with the FBI logo. It looked like the real thing – it even featured an official-looking Freedom of Information Act request form. Many citizens like to request information from the government, and so the presence of such a request form on the website contributed to the perception of its authenticity. Visitors to the website furnished the information requested, including their credit card numbers to pay the ten dollar application fee. Needless to say, no one ever got what they paid for-but they did get plenty of trouble straightening out damaged credit histories.

"Spoofing" or "phishing" is also a growing problem. Using this scam, identity thieves attempt to make Internet users believe they are receiving e-mail from a specific, trusted source, or that they are securely connected to a trusted website. The goal is to convince individuals to provide personal or financial information that enables the perpetrators to commit credit card fraud, bank fraud, or other forms of identity theft.[5]

In one recent scam, a phisher e-mail claiming to be from MSN was sent to computer users. It said: "We regret to inform you that technical difficulties arose with our recent update. Unfortunately part of our customer database and backup system became inactive." This authentic-looking message offered a toll-free telephone number in addition to a web link and urged individuals to click on the link to the phony website. The message then informed individuals that they needed to enter their personal information at the online billing center.[6]

Chat Rooms and Electronic Bulletin Boards

Chat Rooms and electronic bulletin boards have also become breeding grounds for identity theft. When criminals have personal information such as credit card or Social Security numbers that they want to sell, they go to hacker chat rooms or electronic bulletin boards and post messages that they have personal information for sell or trade.

The former employee of an insurance company stole a database containing sixty thousand personnel records and sold some of the private information over the Internet. The suspect posted a message on an electronic bulletin board announcing that he had thousands of names and Social Security numbers for sale. Further investigation revealed that he had also posted the credit card number of a former supervisor.[7]

Just how long does it take for stolen credit cards to find their way around the Internet? About fifteen minutes, according to a fraud investigator who posted phony credit card data in order to track just that. He then listed links to the website in various Internet chat rooms. Within fifteen minutes, seventy-four individuals from thirty-one countries arrived to look at the data.[8]

Information Brokers

Information brokers have been around for decades, furnishing information to attorneys, private investigators, and other licensed professionals. However, a new breed of information broker has emerged in recent years — the kind that sells personal information to anyone requesting it via the Internet. Driven by greed, some information brokers are careless when they receive an order. They fail to verify the identity of the requestor and do little, if any, probing into the intended use of the information.

In one case, an online information broker was sued by the parents of a young woman slain by an Internet stalker. The suit alleges that for a nominal fee the broker sold personal information that led the killer to the victim's place of employment. He then ambushed her as she got into her car after leaving work.

Online Public Records

People-search and genealogy websites have come under fire and some consumers are concerned that personal information online can be used to commit identity theft. Privacy advocates have become extremely concerned about the ease with which people can obtain personal information online. Local, state, and federal governments have began to make public records of all kinds available online. For example, birth and death records have long been available to the public through state offices, but people had to physically visit the courthouse. Now, it can be accessed by computer.

Even criminals are victimized. Law enforcement websites, which list the names, dates of birth, Social Security numbers, heights, and weights of prison inmates and wanted criminals, have become targets for identity thieves. Sometimes, identity thieves are only looking to create false identification so they can obtain credit cards or temporarily impersonate someone else. This technique is attractive because the thief knows just how long it will be before the criminal is released from prison and how much time they have before suspicious account behavior is likely to be recognized.[9]

Johnny May

CHAPTER THREE

How Identity Thieves Steal

Īt is often said that the best offense is a good defense. You must understand the identity thief's mode of operation if you are to successfully defend against an attack. This chapter explores some of the most common techniques used by criminals to steal identities.

Mail Theft

A raised red flag on a mailbox is an open invitation to identity thieves. If a person leaves outgoing bills in the mailbox for the postal carrier to pick up, a thief can use the information to commit identity theft. What's so alarming is that it takes only one stolen item — an outgoing bill or an incoming bank account statement —

for the identity thief to get all the information he or she needs to cause havoc.

A common method of operation employs a process known as check washing, identity thieves erase the ink on a check. Using common household cleaning products such as acetone or bleach, then they rewrite the checks to themselves, often increasing the amount payable by hundreds or thousands of dollars. Mailboxes are generally targeted at the end or the beginning of the month when bills are paid. A thief can steal a check in the morning when the victim leaves for work and cash it by that afternoon. Bank and credit card statements, preapproved credit card offers, telephone calling cards, and drivers license numbers all make attractive targets for the mail thief.

All types of mailboxes are vulnerable. Cluster mailboxes, such as the type found in new subdivisions and apartment complexes, are attractive to thieves because one theft can produce numerous pieces of mail. Suburbs also get hit hard. The individual mailboxes on the street are easily accessed by someone driving a car or walking up and down the street.

Mail carriers have also been victimized. In Los Angeles, gang members discovered that carriers use "arrow keys" to open many of the boxes on their routes — from personal boxes to huge drop-off centers. They began terrorizing the carriers, holding them up at knife and gunpoint, demanding keys and the mail. Ultimately, a cadre of members from the Crips gang extorted twenty-six of the arrow keys. Over a three-year period, they are believed to have stolen letters and parcels in the tens of thousands. In one apartment, authorities found that the gang had stashed $280,000 worth of washed and counterfeit checks. The case prompted an expensive re-keying of the mailboxes.[1]

Fraudulent Address Changes

In this scenario, the criminal fills out a change of address form at the post office so that the victim's mail is redirected to the thief's address or mail drop. The thief then obtains bank and credit card statements or other mail containing the information necessary to take over the victim's identity. Some identity theft rings will even rent inexpensive apartments specifically for the purpose of receiving this mail. Sometimes they will rent an apartment in the victim's name by using a fake identification obtained in the victim's name.[2]

Fortunately, authorities have taken some actions to discourage this activity. For example, identity thieves generally won't use mail forwarding or commercial mailboxes because credit bureau alert programs will identify these addresses. The Postal Service has implemented changes to discourage fraudulent changes of address.

Dumpster Diving (aka Trash Napping)

As the saying goes, one man's trash is another man's treasure! Well, some identity thieves love trash, especially if it is from upscale neighborhoods or business establishments. With a quick call to the sanitation company, thieves can learn the day and time of garbage pickup for the targeted area. Then they usually go to pick through the trash before sunrise. After finding a secluded area to go through their haul, the thieves look for any item that may contain personal identifiers — bank or credit card statements, preapproved credit card offers, and so forth.

Business dumpsters are particularly attractive. Criminals know that these receptacles can contain treasure troves of information about business and customer accounts. Many of these dumpster divers disguise themselves as homeless people. Identity theft ringleaders have been known to hire drug addicts and alcoholics to collect items from the trash.[3] Another common method of trash napping is employed by cleaning crews. They use their access to office and industrial property to secure a steady stream of business trash. In one case, personal information was stolen from 48 patients at a VA medical center and used to establish credit cards and steal thousands of dollars in goods. The thieves apparently reached over counters and into wastebaskets to obtain lists of patient information, including names, addresses, dates of birth, and Social Security numbers.[4]

Businesses most often targeted by trash nappers and dumpster divers include:

- Banks
- Restaurants

- Hotels
- Service Stations
- Travel Agencies
- Pharmacies
- Hospitals
- Airline Ticket Offices

One of the hottest items that divers search for these days is checks — even invalid ones. In one case, a thief went on a spending spree after finding checks from a closed-out account in the trash. It was a case of simple forgery using supposedly worthless checks. Canceled checks are also a prize. The thieves wash the checks using a chemical process that removes the ink from the paper. Or, using an off-the-shelf software package available at most office supply stores, they can scan the canceled check and use computer graphics to clean it up and make it look like new.

Of course, just the account number on the check will suffice. One man, operating out of a California hotel, paid dozens of dumpster divers to sort through trash in search of checking account numbers.[5] After collecting the valid numbers, the thief used his laptop computer to produce checks with altered names. As many law enforcement officials will attest, such checks are not difficult to pass off at stores.

Shoulder Surfing

Anytime you use an ATM or calling card in a public

place you put yourself at risk. Shoulder surfers are criminals who lurk around ATM machines and payphones in high traffic areas such as airports, hotels, and shopping centers. They observe from afar, sometimes using binoculars or camcorders, hoping to catch a glimpse of your personal identification number (PIN) or calling card number. If they get your calling card number, they can sell it on the street. Buyers can use your calling card to make long distance calls for free. With ATM cards, thieves watch and learn the individual's card number and PIN number. Later, they will steal the card or make their own and go back to the ATM to withdraw cash.

Lost or Stolen Purse/Wallet
Old-fashioned pick-pocketing is still a lucrative trade. Nowadays, however, cash is often the last thing that motivates the criminal. A lost or stolen wallet or purse provides the identity thief with a wealth of personal information that he may use to obtain credit or commit crimes in the victim's name. In Texas, a group of thieves moved from city to city, stealing credit cards from victims' purses and then charging thousands of dollars before the victims even knew what had happened.[6]

Insider Access
Surprisingly enough, a lot of times the identity thief is someone from the victim's inner circle — a roommate, relative, client, healthcare provider, and so forth. — who has easy access to the victim's residence and personal

records. In one case, the adult daughter of a Michigan couple obtained credit cards in their names and ran up debts of more than ten thousand dollars. She paid the interest fees to avoid alerting her parents of her use of the cards, but she was not able to keep up with the payments. The credit card companies were able to hold the parents accountable for the bills, given that the debtor was their daughter.

Internet

Identity thieves have also begun to target personal web pages. Many are loaded with information, such as full names, birth dates, addresses, occupations, degrees, and phone numbers. Genealogy fans like to research family trees. They often place details online, such as a mother's maiden name. However, such information is commonly used as a password for credit cards and bank accounts. Therefore, individuals who put such information on their personal or genealogical web pages are increasingly at risk for identity theft.

Keep in mind that anyone, including criminals, can purchase personal information for a nominal fee via the Internet and misuse it to obtain credit in another's name. There are unscrupulous companies that sell all types of personal information.

Skimmers

The advent of easy-to-use skimmers and the Internet has made it easy for criminals to victimize businesses that accept credit cards and ATM debit cards. Smaller than a deck of cards, a skimmer is a device that can read the magnetized strips on bank or credit cards the same way credit card scanners and ATM machines read card information. They can capture and retain information from the cards, including account numbers, balances, and verification codes.

Here is how the scam works. When an unsuspecting customer pays their bill, their card is first swiped through the legitimate card machine, and then secretly it is also swiped through the skimmer machine. The information is then downloaded onto a computer and false cards are made. The cloned card is embossed with the details of the victim's credit card and passed on to others, who may sell the card or use it for their own benefit.[7]

One Christmas, at Bloomingdale's in New York City, an independent vendor in the store's sunglasses department was arrested after she swiped a customer's credit card through a skimmer and transferred its information to a palm-held data organizer.[8] These popular devices can each store thousands of credit card numbers, which can then be printed on bogus cards or e-mailed for use anywhere in the world.

Restaurants are also a place to be on guard. Waiters at two New York restaurants used card skimmers to swipe customer credit cards. In one case, fifteen stolen card numbers added up to a $250,000 shopping spree. Fortunately, the waiters were caught. They were fired and prosecuted.

Pretexting

Sometimes, identity thieves will try to trick others into revealing personal information. One way they do this is by "pretexting," calling under false pretenses, such as contacting banks and posing as the account holder. In other cases, the identity thief may contact the victim directly. For example, in one scheme criminals played on consumer fears about the Y2K computer bug. In this scam, the caller pretended to represent the victim's bank. He either asked the victim to supply certain information about the account or, in another variation, persuaded the victim to transfer money to a special account to ensure the bank could comply with Y2K requirements.[9] Pretexting appears to be gaining popularity in response to the booming market for comprehensive personal information relating to consumers.[10]

Johnny May

CHAPTER FOUR

Prevention Strategies

Society is resorting to innovative approaches to combat this crime. State governments, local and federal law enforcement agencies, and private organizations are all taking new steps to minimize this threat. But it is also vitally important for individuals to take responsibility for protecting their personal information.

The Los Angeles County Sheriff's Department was one of the first law enforcement agencies in the country to create a specialized unit dealing with identity theft. The unit focuses on several areas, including departmentwide training and public education. The unit coordinates its efforts with public and private agencies such as the California Department of Motor Vehicles, credit card companies, and banks. The unit also has developed a guidebook for victims with numbers to call for information and help, as well as guides for field deputies.[1] Police agencies in South Carolina and elsewhere have formed a coalition to educate financial institutions, businesses, and the public about this crime.[2]

Meanwhile, at least one insurance company, the Travelers Property Casualty Corporation, now offers consumers insurance protection for expenses associated with the growing crime of identity theft. The coverage, called Identity Theft Fraud Expense coverage, can be added to a homeowner, condominium, or renters policy for an additional premium of $25 per year and provides $15,000 coverage with a $100 deductible. The coverage reimburses the policyholder for expenses incurred as a result of efforts to clear their name after becoming a victim of identity theft. Covered expenses include legal expenses, loan re-application fees, telephone and certified mailing charges, notary expenses, and lost wages.[3]

Many state governments, agencies, and organizations are taking steps to curb the identity theft epidemic. The following are just a few of those steps:

- California became the first state to create an agency to protect the privacy rights of consumers. The Office of Privacy Protection offers a lot of advice on how to protect your privacy and prevent identity theft. Their website — www.privacyprotection.ca.gov — also provides links to other agencies that can assist with identity theft issues.

- In Georgia, The Georgia Stop Identity Theft Network — www.stopidentitytheft.org — brings together federal, state, and local law enforcement, federal and local prosecutors, corporations, and financial institutions to achieve three primary goals: educate the public and businesses; provide training for law enforcement; and establish a centralized database for victims to report identity theft. The network wants to send a strong message that identity theft will not be tolerated in Georgia.[2]

- In an attempt to prevent identity theft, Visa USA said it will stop merchants that take Visa payments from displaying all but the last four digits of a card number on receipts. The credit card issuer wants all merchants to remove the first twelve digits of the card number and its expiration date from receipts by July 2006.[4]

- The Secret Service is also taking steps to help law enforcement and identity theft victims. They recently released a CD-ROM that serves as an educational and investigative resource to help law enforcement combat identity theft. It includes a ten-minute video designed to be shown at officer roll call meetings. The video provides an overview on identity theft and shares law enforcement officers' experiences in combating this crime. It also includes more than fifty investigative and victim-assistance resources.

Individuals

While no one can guarantee you will not become a victim of identity theft, you can greatly minimize your risk of becoming a victim. Let's look at some safeguards that you can implement.

1. Be extremely cautious when handling and disclosing the following information: Social Security number, mother's maiden name, date of birth, past addresses, driver's license number, and, of course, bank and credit account numbers.

2. Don't voluntarily give out personal information such as credit card numbers or Social Security numbers over the phone unless you initiated the phone call. Ask for a call back number and match it against the telephone book or directory assistance. Check with the Better Business Bureau or other agencies to determine the legitimacy of the business.

3. Invest in a personal shredder. This is your first line of defense. Shred bank and credit card statements, canceled checks, preapproved credit card offers, and so forth before disposal. A cross-cut

shredder offers added security because it makes it harder to reconstruct documents.

4. Place garbage out on the morning of pickup rather than the night before. This gives dumpster divers less opportunity to go through your garbage.

5. Consider listing only your name and phone number in the telephone book or get an unlisted and unpublished number. In your personal listing, avoid the use of professional titles, such as "Dr." or "Attorney," or any other signs announcing you're affluent.

6. Never disclose personal information over a cell or wireless phone.

7. Be aware of other directories in which you may be listed. In addition to the telephone directory (see previous item), criminals have been known to find victims in *Who's Who* and other publications.

8. Purchase a residential mailbox with a locking mechanism or install a mail slot on your door.

9. Have your post office hold your mail while you are on vacation or absent from your home for an extended period of time.

10. Remove your mail from the mailbox as soon as it is delivered, if possible.

11. Consider starting a neighborhood watch program to help keep an eye on mailboxes and report suspected mail thieves.

12. Order checks with extra security features that discourage tampering.

13. Don't leave outgoing checks or paid bills in your residential mailbox. Take your mail to the post office or drop it in a U.S. Postal Service mailbox. Also, consider paying bills electronically; many financial institutions now offer this option.

14. Opt out of preapproved credit card offers by calling (888) 5OPTOUT, or (888) 567-8688. Your request covers all three major credit bureaus (Experian, TransUnion, and Equifax).

15. When you order new checks, do not have them sent to your residence. Pick them up at the bank instead. Or, have them delivered to you by registered mail, so you have to sign for them personally.

16. Call your credit card company if your card has expired and you have not yet received a replacement.

17. Minimize the amount of information you carry in your wallet or purse. Limit the number of credit cards you carry with you and don't carry your Social Security card.

18. To avoid pickpockets, men should carry wallets in a front pocket . Another idea is to place a rubber band around the wallet so it will rub against the cloth, providing an alert that a crime is in progress. You can also place your wallet in your pocket sideways, making it more difficult to get the wallet out of your pocket.

19. Be careful in crowded areas. Pickpockets often deliberately bump or jostle an unsuspecting victim in a crowd as a distraction technique.

20. Don't pat your pocket to see if your wallet is still there. This can alert a pickpocket to the location of your wallet.

21. For women, a purse with a zippered compartment and a flap over the outside is the most secure. Carry the purse with the flap against your body. Avoid drawstring purses.

22. Avoid hanging your purse on the back of a chair in a public place. Place it in your lap.

23. Scrutinize monthly billing statements. Open bills promptly and check your accounts monthly. Look for charges you don't recognize and report them immediately. Report late statements. Save receipts to compare with your billing statements.

24. Contact credit card companies and request that they lower the credit limits on your credit cards to minimize the damage an identity thief can do.

25. Ask your credit card issuers to stop sending unsolicited convenience checks. Identity thieves know the account holder won't see the charges for at least thirty days.

26. When purchasing gas, use a gasoline card instead of a credit card. Gas station attendants and other employees have access to customers names and account numbers even if the card is swiped at the pump. A gasoline card is a lot less attractive to identity thieves.

27. Keep your eyes on your credit card during all transactions (e.g., in restaurants), and get it back as soon as possible.

28. Keep a record of all your credit card account numbers, expiration dates, and the telephone

number and address of each creditor. Store it in a secure place.

29. Be cautious of "shoulder surfers." This crime most often occurs with calling cards. Always shield your calling card number by placing your hand over the telephone keypad, or look for a phone with a card swipe.

30. Order a copy of your credit report at least one or two times per year from each of the three major credit bureaus (Experian, TransUnion, and Equifax). Look for address changes and fraudulent accounts. Check for accuracy. Do this on your birthday to help you remember to do it at least once per year.

31. Consider trying a credit report rotation. Order a copy of your credit report from one of the three major credit bureaus (TransUnion, Experian, Equifax) every four months. Over the course of a year, you will have seen all three of your credit reports.

32. If you think someone has established credit using your child's name, order a copy of their credit report. It is easy to overlook the possibility of fraud involving your child's Social Security number.

33. Ask your creditors to include a security password on your accounts. Stay away from using a mother's maiden name or your Social Security number. While you won't make a lot of points with your creditors, you will provide yourself with an added blanket of security.

34. Cancel credit cards that you seldom use. The more open accounts you have, the more vulnerable you are.

35. Limit the amount of information you place on your Internet home page and on websites detailing family genealogy.

36. Limit the personal information on your checks. Don't preprint your Social Security number, telephone number, or driver's license number on your checks. Disclose it only when absolutely required. If a merchant asks you for your telephone number or driver's license number, you may decide to add it at that time. A retailer should have no need for your Social Security number.

37. Ask your employer and others not to use your Social Security number as an identifier; use an alternative number if possible.

38. Do not allow sales clerks to copy your credit card

numbers onto checks for additional information. It's against the law in some states, and major credit card companies prohibit merchants from charging a customer's credit card account to cover a bad check.

39. Never write down personal identifications numbers (PINs) or passwords; memorize them. Do not use your Social Security number or any easy-to-guess words or number sequences, such as birth dates.

40. When establishing a password, use a combination of numbers, letters, and symbols. Avoid using the same password for other accounts or sites.

41. When ordering online, it is generally preferable to use a credit card (with a low limit) instead of a debit card, because of the immediacy with which a debit card gives a thief access to the cash in your bank account. However, federal law does protect users of both credit and debit cards.

42. If you're interested in doing business online with a company you are not familiar with, ask the company for its physical address and phone number. Use that information to check the business's complaint record with the Better Business Bureau or other consumer protection agencies.

43. Install adequate firewall protection to prevent hackers from accessing personal information stored on your computer.

44. Never give your bank account numbers or Social Security number to online merchants.

45. Before purchasing online, find out if the site has a secure server. Secure pages begin with *https* instead of *http*. A picture of a lock in the locked position should appear on the browser window.

46. If you get an e-mail that warns you, with little or no notice, that an account of yours will be shut down unless you reconfirm your billing information, do not reply or click on the link in the e-mail. Instead, contact the company cited in the e-mail by telephone number or by a website you know to be genuine.

47. You can purchase credit monitoring services that alert you when there are changes in your credit report. Keep in mind, however, that these services usually only cover one of the three major credit bureaus.

48. Notify your credit card companies and financial institutions in advance of any change of address or phone number.

49. Never put your credit card number — or any financial account number — on a postcard or on the outside of an envelope.

50. Quiz organizations, such as banks, brokerages, or employers, about what they do with your private information.

Employers/Businesses

Identity theft in the workplace is on the rise. However, businesses can mimize the risk by taking the proper steps to protect employee and customer information. Let's take a look at some of the safeguards that you can implement.

1. Properly dispose of personal information and other sensitive material. This could be accomplished by shredding documents. Do not allow intact documents to be thrown in dumpsters.

2. Conduct background checks on all individuals with access to personal and/or sensitive information, including personnel from cleaning companies and temporary agencies.

3. Limit the number of temporary agencies your company uses. If possible, maintain the services of one trusted firm.

4. Be sure your cleaning service is licensed and bonded. Do the same with any other contractors that are granted access to your premises.

5. Develop guidelines to safeguard sensitive information; the guidelines should address how to handle such information responsibly.

6. Train staff on information-security issues and include information on the topic in new employee orientations. Educate them on why certain information needs protection and procedures on how to protect it.

7. Promote security awareness through the use of posters, newsletter articles, video presentations, e-mails, and brochures or booklets.

8. Contact your local police department and request a security survey of your facility. Many departments will provide this service free of charge.

9. Limit the use of the Social Security number (SSN) in the workplace. Don't use the number on employee identification badges, time cards, or paychecks. Use alternative numbers.

10. Control access to personal information and limit

it to those employees who have a legitimate reason for access.

11. Secure employees' personal information in a locked file cabinet or other secure area. Sensitive files stored on the computer should be password protected and encrypted.

12. Implement and enforce password security procedures for all computer users. Passwords should be changed on a regularly scheduled basis.

13. Disable employee access to your company's data immediately upon termination.

14. Avoid requesting a Social Security number during the interview phase. If possible, only request it during the hiring phase.

15. Stock relevant publications and audio-visual programs and make them available to company executives and employees.

16. Consider using outside security consultants to assess the vulnerability of your organization's records.

17. Keep audit trails to document and determine who has accessed sensitive personal information.

18. Consider using temporary workers only in areas where they won't have access to sensitive personal information. Instead, rotate an existing employee who has already been screened to fill the temporary position and let the temporary worker fill the existing employee's position.

19. Install adequate firewall protection to prevent hackers from accessing the sensitive personal information stored on your computers.

20. Inform workers or customers when personal information has been compromised.

Johnny May

CHAPTER FIVE

Your Social Security Number

When the Social Security number was created in 1935, Americans were promised that their numbers would not be used as national identification numbers and would only be used to monitor contributions to the federal pension system. In fact, Social Security cards used to be marked "not for identification purposes." Today, the Social Security number has become ubiquitous. Employers display Social Security numbers on name badges, parking permits, and personnel records. College professors post grades by Social Security numbers in an attempt to protect student privacy. (What an irony!)

Consider these other places Social Security numbers are posted or displayed:

- Military ID cards
- Medicare cards
- College ID cards
- Checking and savings account statements
- College and alumni records
- Insurance records
- Tax returns
- Credit bureau header reports

Unfortunately the list could go on and on.

The truth is, anyone can steal your identity and ruin your credit rating and reputation. All they need is your Social Security number. Then why is this number so readily available? The answer is convenience. Businesses know that phone numbers, addresses, and even names change, but Social Security numbers, for the most part, do not.

Until Internet use became commonplace, the concern about Social Security numbers and threats to personal privacy remained relatively minimal. The P-Trak controversy in 1996 helped to change that by demonstrating that personal identifiers, such as Social Security numbers, were being sold through online services. Created by Lexis-Nexis, this online service allowed individuals to enter a name and receive the corresponding Social Security number. The program created such an outcry that the company suspended this program's search capability within two weeks of its introduction.

What Do Those Numbers Mean?

Every Social Security number has nine digits. The first three digits represent the state where the card was issued. The middle two digits have no special significance; they merely serve to break the numbers into blocks of convenient size. The last four digits of a Social Security number represent a straight numerical progression of assigned numbers. These last four digits are commonly used by banks and credit card companies to enable customers to access account information over the phone. So it's really the last four digits that identify an individual.[2]

SSN and Credit Header Information

What is the credit header? It's the identifying information that accompanies a consumer's credit reports. It consists of name, name variations, addresses, former addresses, telephone numbers, date of birth, and Social Security number. The credit header data is sold separately from the credit history and is widely used by private investigators, skip tracers, attorneys, information brokers, and other groups who specialize in locating individuals — including those whose purpose is identity theft.

Legislation has been proposed to limit the use of credit header information. U.S. Senator Diane Feinstein, D-Calif., introduced a bill that would limit the use of Social Security numbers by prohibiting commercial acquisition, distribution, and use of the numbers without permission. Specifically, it would prevent credit card companies and other such agencies from selling header information to other companies. It would also prevent any state's department of motor vehicles from giving out personal information for surveys or solicitors.

How the SSN Causes Problems

In the wrong hands, the Social Security number can wreak havoc. For example, a desk clerk at a Florida college spent over $100,000 using credit cards he acquired with student Social Security numbers. By the time the clerk was caught, he had used the stolen identities to purchase stereos, computer printers, televisions, a riding lawnmower, and a washing machine.

In 1967, the military made the decision to use the Social Security number as a military serial number. Access to this information enabled a prisoner at a federal penitentiary in Missouri to turn his assignment to a clothing room into a lucrative scam. His job was to sort out army fatigues from Fort Leonard Wood. As a long-time veteran of tax fraud, it didn't take him long to figure out that the uniforms were a potential gold mine: On each piece of clothing was a soldier's name and Social Security number.

The identity thief requested blank tax forms by mail and filed phony tax returns and requests for refunds, using the names and Social Security numbers he'd copied from the uniforms. This generated more than 200 refund checks mailed to addresses selected by the criminal. The IRS discovered the fraud and was able to stop many of the refund checks. Nevertheless, the Army continued to send old uniforms with Social Security numbers and names on each piece to the federal detention facility.[1]

The military's use of the Social Security number as an identifier also caused a retired air force colonel and his wife to become the victims of identity theft. Out of the blue, the couple received a call demanding payment on a Jeep Cherokee. The only problem was the couple didn't own a Jeep Cherokee. They later found out someone 1500 miles away had used the colonel's Social Security number and good credit to purchase the jeep. It didn't stop there. Their credit report revealed that five cars had been purchased using their Social Security numbers, including another Jeep Cherokee, a Ford Ranger pickup truck, a 1988 Ford Bronco, and a 1995 Plymouth Neon. In all, a total of thirty-three separate fraudulent accounts were opened in their names, totaling $113,000.[3]

When Should You Give Out Your Social Security number?
Government agencies face restrictions on the use of Social Security numbers. The Privacy Act of 1974 requires all government agencies — federal, state and local- that use your Social Security number to provide you with a disclosure statement. The statement tells whether you're required to provide your Social Security number or whether it's optional, how the Social

Security number will be used, and what will happen if you refuse to provide it. If you are asked to give the number to a government agency and no disclosure statement is included on the form, complain and cite the Privacy Act.[4]

You are not compelled by law to disclose your Social Security number to private organizations. You may choose not to supply your Social Security number, but, by the same token, a private organization may refuse you its goods or services. Keep in mind that the IRS requires employers to obtain the Social Security number of each person they employ.

Banks are required by the IRS to report the Social Security number of account holders to whom they pay interest.

Johnny May

CHAPTER SIX

False Identification

A major weapon in the identity thief's arsenal is false identification. With a fake driver's license and social security card, a person with no financial background can easily establish bank accounts, purchase goods, and obtain credit cards using someone else's identity. Most types of identity theft involve false identification at some point or another. The following documents are commonly counterfeited or fraudulently obtained:

- Social Security cards
- state driver's licenses
- passports/visas
- voter registration cards

Technology

Today's identity thieves are not armed with knives or guns, but high-tech desktop publishing equipment. Some law enforcement authorities attribute the increase in fraudulent identification use to the availability of inexpensive office products and computer graphics programs. The current technology makes it possible to produce high-quality false identification documents.

In San Francisco, an identity theft ring specializing in mail theft used a variety of computers and color printers to generate phony identifications from the documents they had stolen. The ring was ultimately traced and caught after police determined that the counterfeiting was being done with a specialized color printer, which required a particular cartridge available only in certain computer supply stores.[1] Hundreds of fraudulent driver's licenses, replicas of credit and ATM cards, and numerous fake checks were confiscated by the police. Thousands of dollars worth of equipment, including digital cameras, hologram imprinting devices, PCs, printers, and scanners were seized.

In a separate case, two Florida men targeted a dozen central Florida dealerships and drove out with $500,000 worth of luxury late-model cars, boats, and trucks — all in someone else's name. The identity thieves created fake driver's licenses using stolen information from retirees all over the country. According to officials, the duo had someone on the inside of a business obtain personal information on retirees in six states.[2]

Problems at the DMV

Break-ins have become a problem for many department of motor vehicle offices. In Washington, an identity theft ring burglarized various state licensing offices twenty-eight times over a two-year period. In five of the break-ins, thieves stole equipment, including cameras, plates, and laminates. In separate thefts, they stole purses and wallets. Then they made fake licenses with their own photos and the information from the stolen credit cards, licenses, and checkbooks. Not only did they make purchases on the stolen credit cards and checks, but they used the false identification to open new bank accounts and obtain new credit cards.[3]

Bribery at many motor vehicle departments has also become a problem. This is due in part to the high volume of low-paid employees. In one case, a former department of motor vehicles employee allegedly accepted bribes to issue regular driver's licenses, commercial driver's license, and state ID cards based on falsified or fictitious information and altered test results.[4]

Counterfeit or Fraudulent?

Counterfeit documents are intended to convey that the document is a genuine identification document, such as a driver's license or social security card. Thieves use desktop publishing equipment to create such documents with stolen information.

Fraudulently obtained documents are genuine documents obtained under the names of other people.5 For example, a fraudulent driver's license is created when someone completes an application for a driver's license using either someone else's personal information or presenting false information. A fraudulent license can also be otained by paying off a worker at the licensing bureau.[6]

There are ID scanners that can read the magnetic strips or bar codes on the back of licenses and other identification. After the information is read, it is then sent to a screen that displays the name, address, and other information about the cardholder. Not every state has the same standard for licenses. There is no national standard in terms of how information is encoded, the different types of information that are encoded in the license itself, and the ways in which it can be read by different ID scanners.[7]

False ID Websites

Lawmakers have also cracked down on websites selling ID templates. The federal Internet False Identification Prevention Act of 2000 makes it a felony for websites based in the United States to offer templates for fake driver's licenses. Those who violate the act can be sentenced to a year in prison if their template is used to make even one ID. The potential punishment escalates up to twenty years if a template is used for more than five fake IDs.[8]

Sites walk around the law by being based in other

countries or using disclaimers. They refer to their products as novelty items or souvenirs — not intended to be
passed off as legitimate identification.[9]

Johnny May

CHAPTER SEVEN

If You Become a Victim

How do you know you've become a victim of identity theft? Here are some red flags or indicators.

- You are denied credit.
- A new or renewed credit card never arrives in the mail.
- You start receiving calls from creditors about debts you have no knowledge of.
- You discover unauthorized purchases on your billing statements.

What to Do

If someone has stolen your identity, the FTC recommends that you take four actions immediately:

1. Contact the fraud department of any one of the three major credit bureaus to place a fraud alert on your credit report. The fraud alert requests creditors to contact you before opening any new accounts or making any changes to your existing accounts. As soon as the credit bureau confirms your fraud alert, the other two credit bureaus will be automatically notified to place fraud alerts, and all three credit reports will be sent to you free of charge. Once you receive your reports, review them carefully to make sure no fraudulent accounts have been opened in your name or unauthorized changes made to your existing accounts.

Reporting Fraud to Credit Bureaus		
Credit Bureau	To Report Fraud	To Order Credit Report
Equifax (www.equifax.com)	(800) 525-6285	(800) 685-1111
Experian (www.experian.com)	(888) 397-3742	(888) 397-3742
Trans Union (www.transunion.com)	(800) 680-7289	(800) 888-4213

2. Contact the creditors (credit card companies, banks, and other lenders) and close any accounts that you know or believe have been tampered with or opened fraudulently. Ask to speak with someone in the security or fraud department of each creditor. It's particularly important to notify credit card companies in writing.

3. File a police report. Get a copy of the report to submit to your creditors and others that may require proof of the crime.

4. File a complaint with the FTC. The FTC maintains a database of identity theft cases. Law enforcement agencies use the database for investigations. Filing a complaint also helps the agency learn more about identity theft and the problems victims are facing. Your complaint helps them better assist everyone.[1]

You can also fill out the FTC's ID Theft Affidavit. (See appendix F.) It is a single affidavit that dozens of banks and other financial institutions have agreed to accept, simplifying the process of alerting companies where a new account was opened in the victim's name.[2] Developed by the FTC in conjunction with banks, credit issuers, and consumer advocates, the ID Theft Affidavit is accepted by participating credit issuers, retailers, banks, and other financial institutions.

Follow-up Steps

It takes time and persistence to regain your creditworthiness. Be prepared to follow up and even follow up again. Here are some basic considerations.

- Once you have received your credit reports, check them for accuracy. Look for accounts you don't recognize or unauthorized changes made to your existing account. Continue to check your credit reports periodically, especially in the first year of discovery, to make sure no new fraudulent activity has occurred. Also, check information such as your Social Security number, address, name, and variations of your name including initials, for accuracy.

- When you call the toll-free fraud number of any of the three major credit bureaus to place a fraud alert on your credit report, remember, the automated "one call" process only works for the initial placement of your fraud alerts. Orders for additional credit reports or renewals of your fraud alerts must be made separately at each of the three major credit bureaus.

- Don't pay any disputed bills. This can be considered a legal admission that the debts actually belong to you.

- Do *not* cancel your unaffected credit cards — that is, the ones that the thieves missed. Because your credit has been tarnished or destroyed, you may have problems when you attempt to open new lines of credit. Keep what you can!

- If someone has tampered with your existing

accounts, close the account and open a new one. Establish a new personal identification number (PIN) or password when you open the new account.

- Be persistent if police will not take a report. If you can't get the local police to take a report, try the county or state police.

- Victims can request that credit bureaus place a fraud alert on their credit report. This is no guarantee against future fraud, because the alerts may not be displayed prominently enough to draw the attention of creditors. Creditors often order credit scores as opposed to an entire credit report, and information of the fraud alert is never forwarded.

Your Liability

Your liability varies depending on the circumstances. For example, if someone uses your ATM or debit card to fraudulently withdraw money from your bank account, the Electronic Funds Transfer Act limits your losses to $50 if you report the theft within two business days after receiving a bank statement that includes an unauthorized transfer. If you report the loss between two and sixty days after discovering the loss, you can be liable for up to $500 of what a criminal withdraws. If you wait more than sixty days, the law doesn't require your bank to reimburse you for any losses. However, you are not responsible for any losses after you inform the bank that your ATM or debit card is lost or stolen.[2]

Visa and Mastercard have voluntarily agreed to limit consumer liability for unauthorized use of their debit cards in most instances to $50 per card, no matter how much time has elapsed since the discovery of the loss or theft of the card. If your credit card is used fraudulently, your liability is limited to $50 per card under the Fair Credit Billing Act. However, Visa and Mastercard have recently adopted zero liability policies. The act also establishes procedures for resolving billing errors on your credit card accounts.

While no federal law limits your losses if someone steals your checks and forges your signature, state laws may protect you. Most states hold the bank responsible for losses from a forged check. At the same time, most states require you to take reasonable care of your account. Contact your state banking or consumer protection agency.

Under the Fair Credit Reporting Act, you have the right to dispute inaccurate information contained within your credit file. The credit bureaus must conduct an investigation if you inform them of incorrect information. If you disagree with the results of the investigation, you may add a brief statement to your file, detailing your version of what actually occurred.

The Importance of Documentation

Document everything! Keep a detailed log of everything

you do in your dealings with creditors, investigators, law enforcement authorities, and so forth. Maintain copies of letters and documents and send all correspondence by certified mail. Keep a record of phone conversations. Make sure those records include:

- name of the person you spoke with;
- time and date of the call;
- phone number; and
- topic of discussion.

The following is a list of key documents you should keep on file:[3]

- police report;
- chronological and detailed journal of events;
- any applications, credit slips, credit cards, or other physical proof of fraud;
- credit reports;
- telephone records;
- costs;
- copies of all letters you send or receive regarding the case;
- all court documents;
- victim statements;
- court notes; and
- summary of case to date.

Checking and savings accounts: If you have reason to

believe that an identity thief has accessed your checking or savings account, close the accounts immediately and obtain new account numbers. If you have had checks stolen or bank accounts set up fraudulently, report it to the following check verification companies:

- International Check Services (800) 631-9656
- Certegy, Inc. (800) 437-5120
- TeleCheck (800) 710-9898
- Scan (800) 262-7771

Stop payment on any outstanding checks you are unsure of. If your ATM card has been lost, stolen, or compromised, cancel the card and get another with a new PIN. Ask for a secret password that must be used before every transaction.

Additional Considerations

- Notify the passport office that you have been the victim of identity theft. Tell them to be on the lookout for anyone ordering a passport fraudulently using your name and identification. Call or write the U.S. Department of State, Passport Services, Consular Lost/Stolen Passport Section, 1111 19th Street, NW, Suite 500, Washington, D.C., 20036, (202) 955-0292.

- Contact your state's department of motor vehicles

if you know or suspect your driver's license number has been compromised and order a copy of your driving record. Ask for an alternate number if your state uses your Social Security number as your driver's license number. You can also request that your files be flagged for possible fraud.

- Notify postal inspectors if you suspect mail fraud.

- If you know or suspect your Social Security number has been used to file federal income tax returns or commit other tax fraud, contact the Internal Revenue Service at (800) 829-0433 or visit their website (www.treas.gov/irs/ci/).

- If an identity thief has filed for bankruptcy using your name, you must file a complaint with the U.S. Trustee in the region where the bankruptcy was filed. Check www.usdoj.gov/ust for a complete listing of U.S. Trustee Program offices. Write a letter explaining someone filed bankruptcy using your name. You must provide proof of your identity.

- If your securities investments or brokerage accounts have been compromised, contact your broker or representative immediately and file a complaint with the Securities Exchange Commission (SEC). SEC Complaint Center, 450 Fifth

Street, NW, Washington, DC 20549-0213, (202) 942-7040.

- Contact your utility companies (gas, water, electric, and telephone) as well if you suspect fraudulent activity.

- If your Social Security number has been used fraudulently to obtain Social Security benefits, report the problem to the Social Security Administration Fraud Hotline at (800) 269-0271. You may order your Earnings and Benefits Statement by calling (800) 772-1213. The Social Security Administration also investigates cases that involve the use of counterfeit Social Security cards, the manufacturing and selling of counterfeit Social Security cards, and the selling of legitimate Social Security cards or information. It does not deal with cases in which your Social Security number has been used in other types of situations, such as purchases.

- If someone has created a criminal record using your name, contact the arresting or citing law enforcement agency. In some cases, you may require the assistance of an attorney.

Johnny May

CHAPTER EIGHT

Identity Theft in the Workplace

Recent headlines have shed light on a growing problem: individuals who illegally retrieve and sell personal information that a business has collected for legitimate reasons. Consider the following:

- A former help-desk worker used his position at a company that performs credit checks to obtain the personal information of thousands of individuals. The worker allegedly conspired with an accomplice to sell the victims' credit reports to an identity theft ring. The ring supplied the pair with the names and Social Security numbers of the individuals whose identities they wanted to steal. The worker, who had left the help-desk position two years earlier, allegedly used codes he had obtained then to access credit reports. He was also accused of providing access codes and passwords to at least one cohort, who then used the codes to obtain consumer credit reports.[1]

- A ring of identity thieves targeted a group of high-ranking executives. A temporary employee working at a company's world headquarters obtained personal information about company executives and then sold it. The information, including Social Security numbers and birthdates, was used to obtain credit cards. The police estimated about $100,000 was charged to the cards.[2]

- The former employee of an insurance company stole a database containing 60,000 personnel records and sold some of the private information over the Internet. The suspect posted a message on an electronic bulletin board announcing that he had thousands of names and Social Security numbers for sale. Further investigation revealed he had also posted the credit card number of a former supervisor. At the same time, he allegedly created false e-mail addresses and sent harassing messages to colleagues.[3]

Personnel Files

So how does this happen? An individual can do everything right, from shredding documents that contain sensitive personal information to monitoring credit reports, but the reality is your personal information is only as safe as the organization protecting it.

TransUnion, one of the three major credit bureaus, has identified theft of records from employers or other businesses as the leading underlying cause of credit fraud and identity theft.[4] According to the Federal Trade Commission, about 90 percent of business record thefts involve payroll or employment records, while only about 10 percent are customer lists.[5] Employers maintain a wealth of information on hundreds, or even thousands, of individuals, including current and past employees, as well as job applicants. If an individual taps into an organization's personnel files, it's a home run for the identity thief.

Identity theft rings have been known to recruit employees who have access to personnel records, credit reports, or other sources of personal information. Identity theft rings pay individuals anywhere from $20-$60 for an identity. In one case, a Wisconsin bank teller sold lists of customer financial records to an identity theft ring.[6] Individuals in identity theft rings have also been known to apply for jobs that will give them access to personal information. One major problem with incidents of this nature is some organizations try to avoid potential embarrassment and negative publicity by not informing employees or customers that their personal information may have been compromised.

In another separate case, a teacher at a middle school

complained to a colleague when bill collectors started calling him at work. Another teacher who had also been victimized overheard him. When they began to inquire, they soon found that several teachers had been the victims of identity theft. After checking credit records four teachers found they had the same fraudulent address on their credit reports. The identity thieves had also applied for the same card on every teacher's record.

Employer Liability

Times have changed and organizations can no longer take a head-in-the-sand approach to identity theft. The issue of employer liability in cases of workplace identity theft is becoming an issue. In California, the employees of a pharmaceutical company sued for negligence when a lab worker came across a box of personnel records in a storage closet. The lab worker and her acquaintances fraudulently rented apartments, opened cell phone accounts, and established more than twenty-five credit card accounts, which they used to purchase $100, 000 in goods. The company settled out of court.[7]

Whether or not a company can be held legally responsible for negligence depends on the degree of reasonable care you afford to employees' personal information. Consider two scenarios. In the first, employee records are left out in the open. In the second, the files are stored in a locked cabinet. The first scenario might support a claim of employer neglect; the second probably would not.[8]

Georgia has one of the nation's toughest laws requiring businesses to protect consumer information. The state's law requires all businesses to destroy private information – Social Security numbers, health records, financial documents and other information – before disposing of it. The information must be shredded, burned, or rendered unreadable.[9]

California has passed a law that limits the use of Social Security numbers to identify customers. Under SB 168 California companies cannot:

- post or display Social Security numbers;

- print Social Security numbers on identification cards or badges;

- print a Social Security numbers on anything mailed to a customer unless it's required by law or the document is a form or application;

- require people to transmit a Social Security number over the Internet unless the connection is secure or the number is encrypted; or

- require people to log on to a website using a Social Security number without a password.

However, the California law has several exceptions:

- The law does not apply if state or federal law requires a Social Security number on a document. That means Social Security numbers will still appear on federal and state tax forms and employee stubs.

- Private schools and colleges have to comply, but public ones don't.

- Companies may still use Social Security numbers to identify customers internally.[10]

Used PCs have also been known to contain sensitive information. In one case, an individual purchased a used laptop at a liquidation auction. When he booted up the computer, on the hard drive he found a folder containing sensitive data from a defunct network software company. The file contained the Social Security numbers and salaries of at least forty-six employees, payroll information, employee termination letters, extensive minutes from executive and board meetings, and documents outlining strategic plans.[11] So remember, always give your computers a meticulous cleaning before placing them on the auction block.

Johnny May

CHAPTER NINE

Identity Theft
Case Files

Let's briefly examine some more cases of identity theft. By understanding what has happened to identity theft victims, you can better protect yourself.

Mail Theft in Colorado

A group of Colorado apartment complexes had more than five hundred mailboxes broken into by mail thieves over a period of one month. The thieves used a screwdriver or some other tool to pry open the mailboxes at the apartment buildings. One resident discovered her $22 credit card payment had been removed from her mailbox, washed, and cashed for $800 at a local bank.[1]

Airport Credit Card Scam

Travelers passing through Vancouver International Airport lost hundreds of thousands of dollars to a credit card scam operating at the international gate. When travelers were informed that they had to pay an airport improvement fee — it was indeed a legitimate fee — they turned over their credit cards. The criminals would then double swipe the credit cards, once through the legitimate machine and once through an illegal device that recorded the credit card account number. The travelers had no idea what had occurred. Once the credit card number was recorded, it was downloaded and reproduced on a fake card and used for various purchases. Police were alerted by a credit card company concerned with a high number of abnormal charges. The company noticed the abnormal charges appeared after the airport improvement fee had been paid.[2]

ID Theft at the DMV

Several employees at a department of motor vehicles were allegedly bribed to "clean" car titles, alter the vehicle identification numbers on cars, and in some cases create new identities. One employee allegedly took payments of $150 to $200. In exchange, the employee issued state identifications or driver's licenses to applicants who lacked the required documentation. The employee also falsified or altered information in the records, including dates of birth, Social Security numbers, and addresses. The employee also created illegal titles for cars that were stolen or that had been resold after being involved in serious accidents.[3]

Big Fish at the FTC

Of all the credit card numbers in the world, a thief stole one belonging to Robert Pitofsky, a top federal regulator of the credit card industry and the chairman of the Federal Trade Commission.[4] Pitofsky disclosed that someone stole his official government credit card in 1998 and ran up charges buying mail order items from catalogs.

Lone Star Credit Demon

When a Wisconsin woman and her husband went to the bank to refinance their home, they thought it would be routine. They were refinancing with their existing mortgage lenders, and they had good credit — or so they thought. They were shocked when the bank officer turned them down and pointed to their credit report. A woman in Texas had applied for credit nineteen times using the victim's name and Social Security number. She made purchases totaling $60,000.[5]

Relative Steals Woman's Identity

After her military clearance was suddenly suspended, an army employee discovered that a relative had stolen her identity and opened several fraudulent accounts. In an effort to clear herself, she paid off $30,000 in fraudulent debts. She then quit her job for a better-paying one, but the offer was subsequently withdrawn after the prospective employer saw her credit report. As a result, she was left jobless and unable to maintain her apartment. Ultimately, she had to leave the country because the only employment she was able to obtain was in Korea.[6]

$250,000 Spending Spree

One identity thief was opening bank accounts under several identities — usually with stolen driver's licenses and Social Security numbers. He then deposited stolen or forged checks, withdrawing some or all of the money before the check cleared. Every month or so, he'd move on to a new alias and a new checking account. The FBI was investigating one alias and the Secret Service was investigating another; they didn't know they were investigating the same person. The criminal was eventually caught, putting an end to his $250,000 spending spree.[7]

Precautions Were Not Enough

A thirty-four-year-old surgeon had her purse stolen from a locked desk at the hospital where she was employed. She quickly canceled her credit cards and checks. About two years later she received a phone call from a collection agency about an overdue account of $3,500 from an out-of-state jewelry store. A copy of her credit report revealed that almost $30,000 worth of jewelry, roaming cell phone charges, and department store charges had been made in her name.[8]

Trafficking in New Credit Card Accounts

One afternoon a California woman was feeding her

one-year-old daughter when the telephone rang. The credit card company informed her someone had applied for a credit card in her name, and it didn't match the addresses they had for her. Someone had already used the credit card, acquired over the Internet without her knowledge, to make almost $500 in unauthorized purchases. Months passed, and soon she discovered more than three dozen of her former co-workers at a pharmaceuticals company had also become victims of identity theft. The group discovered that their identities were used to illegally obtain about seventy-five credit cards, buy at least $100,000 in merchandise, open twenty cellular telephone accounts, and rent three apartments.[9]

Will the Real Mother Please Pay the Bill?

A Florida woman was recently charged with assuming a former neighbor's identity and insurance when she admitted herself into a hospital for the delivery of her baby. The victim, a Texas woman, contacted police after receiving a series of phone calls from a Florida hospital demanding payment for delivery of her child. The accused also had opened utilities and bank accounts in the victim's name.[10]

Does Grandma Really Need All Those Phones?

Seniors are often the target of identity thieves. Creditors were shocked to learn that the purported owner of five Nextel phones was an infirm, ninety-three-year-old woman who required around-the-clock care.[11]

The Enterprising Data Entry Clerk

A data entry clerk in Tampa, Florida, who had access to sensitive personal information was accused of stealing the identities of 350 people. The woman was arrested after trying to make a fraudulent purchase with a credit card. Inside her car, police found what they described as 350 "complete identities," including victim names, addresses, Social Security numbers, and dates of birth.[12]

Identity Theft Murder

In Detroit, a woman was actually murdered in a bizarre case of identity theft. The perpetrator, a woman with a troubled past, had been a co-worker of the victim. This identity thief hired her nephew and a friend to kill the victim — but changed the dead woman's identity to her own. When police found the victim's body, the perpetrator persuaded them that she was the victim's sister! The scheme unraveled a couple days later when police brought the identity thief's relatives to the funeral home and they did not recognize the dead woman.[13]

Preying on Cancer Patients

A former employee at one of the country's leading cancer centers was recently charged with stealing the Social Security numbers and other information she gathered from patients. The woman worked for about four months after being hired through a temporary agency. The center sent a mass mailing to 12,000 people who were admitted for treatment while the woman was working there, suggesting that they check their credit reports.[14]

Identity Theft Puts Golf Star "in the Rough"

Tiger Woods had to go to trial to protect his good name. Prosecutors charged Anthony Lemar Taylor of Sacramento, California, with using the golf superstar's real name — Eldrick T. Woods — and Social Security number to apply for credit cards and obtain a fake driver's license. The perpetrator ran up $17,000 in credit card charges before police identified Taylor as the suspect.[15]

Moonlighting at the Morgue

Ten morgue workers in Philadelphia were charged with stealing cash, credit cards, weapons, and bank and personal information from dead people. Six accomplices were also charged, because they allegedly benefited from the thefts by processing the stolen credit cards and opening new accounts in the names of the deceased. The investigation was prompted when a woman discovered that someone had used her dead father's credit cards and opened new accounts in his name.[16]

Identity Thieves Target Fitness Club Parking Lots

An identity theft ring stole credit cards, driver's licenses, passports, and checks from at least three hundred vehicles after fitness club members left their wallets and purses unattended in their cars while they worked out in the health club.[17]

Man Steals Identities of Nation's Top Executives

A man stole the identities of some of the nation's top executives to buy $730,000 in diamonds and rolex watches. The man allegedly identified prominent business executives by reading *Who's Who in America*. He then called banks and credit card companies, impersonated victims, and persuaded the companies to change billing addresses on the accounts to hotels in Tennessee, Arkansas, and Mississippi. He used the financial information to purchase jewelry from New York and other cities.[18]

Not Even Jail Can Stop a Determined Criminal

A convict already serving a nine-year sentence was charged with identity theft. Authorities said the man used telephones and the mail at the correctional facility to carry out the scheme. The man and five accomplices, including his girlfriend, allegedly used contacts at businesses to commit fraud, purchase cars, and open checking accounts.[19]

Identity Theft Victim's Children Taken

A pregnant woman checked into a hospital using another woman's ID and gave birth. The woman then disappeared. Doctors later determined the baby was sick because the mother had used crack, so they gave her name to child protective services. The name actually belonged to someone who was the victim of identity theft. Child protective services held the victim's two children, believing she was the one who gave birth at the hospital. It took the woman several humiliating hours to get her children back.[20]

Employees Awaken the Dead to Steal Benefits

A senior congressional liason in the Veteran's Administration Office allegedly used her authority to reactivate the files of veterans who had died without beneficiaries. According to investigators, the perpetrator increased the veterans' disability to 100 percent, made them eligible for long-term retroactive benefits, and made the revived accounts payable to a co-conspirator.[21]

Three Stooges Firm Used in Scam

Over a period of several years, an identity thief used variations of the Three Stooges ficticious law firm "Dewey, Cheetum, and Howe" to obtain cashiers checks from banks. The criminal was caught when a banker became suspicious about the company name and contacted the FBI. The one-man operation bilked credit card companies and gambling casinos out of one million dollars.[22]

Johnny May

Credit Bureaus

Requesting Credit Reports and Reporting Fraud

There are three major credit bureaus that maintain credit history on consumers. You should contact these organizations when you wish to get a copy of your credit report or if you have questions about your credit history. There is often a fee for this service. However, if you have been denied credit, you are entitled by law to receive a free credit report from each credit bureau. Also, the law now requires that victims of identity theft receive free annual credit reports.

Equifax
Order credit report: (800) 685-1111
Report fraud: (800) 525-6285
Website: www.equifax.com

Experian
Order credit report: (888) 397-3742
Report fraud: (888) 397-3742
Website: www.experian.com

TransUnion
Order credit report: (800) 888-4213
Report fraud: (800) 680-7289
Website: www.transunion.com

Letter Requesting Removal from Marketing Lists
On the following page is a sample letter that can be used to ask these bureaus to refrain from selling your name and address to advertisers.

Date:

To whom it may concern:

I request to have my name removed from your marketing lists. Following is the information you have asked me to include in my request.

My first, middle, and last name are:
(*List all name variations, including Jr., Sr., etc.*)

My current mailing address is:

My previous mailing address is:
(*Fill in your previous mailing address if you have moved in the last six months.*)
Note: not required by Equifax and Experian.

My Social Security number is:
Note: not required by Experian.

My date of birth is:
Note: not required by Equifax and Experian.

Thank you for your prompt handling of my request.

_____

Signature

Resources

The organizations, publications, and websites in this appendix have information or perform services that can be helpful to victims of identity theft. They all provide information about prevention strategies.

Organizations

Identity Theft Data Clearinghouse
Federal Trade Commission
600 Pennsylvania Avenue, NW
Washington, DC 20580
Phone: (877)-IDTHEFT
Website: www.consumer.gov/idtheft

Direct Marketing Association
1120 Avenue of Americas
New York, NY 10036-6700
Phone: (212) 768-7277
Website: www.the-dma.org

CALPIRG
1107 9th St, Suite 601
Sacramento, CA 95814
Phone: (916) 448-4516
E-mail: info@calpirg.org
Website: www.calpirg.org

Identity Theft Prevention and Survival
28202 Cabot Road, Suite 300
Laguna Niguel, CA 92677
Contact: Mari J. Frank, Esq., Author, *The Identity Theft Survival Kit*
Phone (800) 725-0807 or (949) 364-1511
Website: www.identitytheft.org

Privacy Rights Clearinghouse
3100 5th Ave., Suite B
San Diego, CA 92103
Contact: Director, Beth Givens
Phone: (619) 298-3396
E-mail: prc@privacyrights.org
Website: www.privacyrights.org

Identity Theft Resource Center
PO Box 26833
San Diego, CA 92196
Contact: Linda Foley, Executive Director
Phone: (858) 693-7935
E-mail: itrc@idtheftcenter.org
Website: www.idtheftcenter.org

Publications

Privacy Times
PO Box 302
Cabin John, MD 20818
Phone: (301) 229-7002
E-mail: evan@privacytimes.com
Website: www.privacytimes.com

Privacy Journal
PO Box 28577
Providence, RI 02908
Phone: 401-274-7861
e-mail: orders@privacyjournal.net
Website: www.privacyjournal.net

Identity Theft: The Cybercrime of the Milennium
by John Q. Newman
Loompanics Unlimited
PO Box 1197
Port Townsend, WA 98368
Website: www.loompanics.com

From Victor to Victim: A Step-by-Step Guide for Ending the Nightmare of Identity Theft
by Mari Frank
Porpoise Press
28202 Cabot Road, Suite 215
Laguna Niguel, CA 92677
Website: www.identitytheft.org

Identity Theft: How to Protect Your Most Valuable Asset
by Robert Hammond
Career Press
3 Tice Road, PO Box 687
Franklin Lakes, NJ 07417
Website: www.careerpress.com

Identity Theft
by John R. Vacca
Prentice Hall PTR
Upper Saddle River, NJ 07458
Website: www.phptr.com

Video

How to Protect Your Credit, Your Money
and Your Good Name
Crime Prevention Resources
33 North Central Ave., Suite 219
Medford, OR 97501
Phone: (800) 867-0016
Website: www.crimeprevent.com

Identity Theft Websites

Identity Theft Prevention Information:
www.identitytheftinfo.com

Privacy Rights Clearinghouse: www.privacyrights.org

Identity Theft Prevention & Survival: www.identi-
tytheft.org

Federal Trade Commission Identity Theft Information:
www.consumer.gov/idtheft/

U.S. Department of Justice: Identity Theft & Fraud:
www.usdoj.gov/criminal/fraud/idtheft.html

Identity Theft Resource Center: www.idtheftcenter.org

Fight Identity Theft: www.fightidentitytheft.com

Identity Theft Protection:
www.identity-theft-protection.com

National Fraud Center: www.nfcglobal.com

Victims of Credit Reporting: www.vcr.org

About Identity Theft: www.aboutidentitytheft.com

How to Protect Your Identity:
www.securemyidentity.com

101 Identity Theft: www.101-identitytheft.com

Johnny May

Check Verification Companies

If you have had any checks stolen or had bank accounts set up fraudulently, report it to these check verification companies:

- SCAN: (800) 262-7771
- Certigy: (800) 437-5120
- International Check Service: (800) 631-9656
- TeleCheck: (800) 710-9898

Johnny May

Notarized
Affadavit

WITNESSETH:

I, _____ being of sound mind and body hereby depose and say:

(1) I reside at _____ (address), _____ (city-state-zip), and that my Social Security number is _____. I was born on _____.

(2) I did not use, nor did I authorize anyone else to use, my name or identification to apply for credit or make charges on said credit obtained unlawfully.

(3) I hereby agree to cooperate with your fraud unit and any law

enforcement agency in the prosecution of the individual who applied for credit and used that credit in my name without authorization, and in any civil action which may be brought to recover damages.

IN WITNESS WHEREOF, I hereunto set my hand this _____ day of _____, _____

Signed _____,

STATE OF _____ COUNTY OF _____

- -

I,_____, residing in the county and state aforesaid, do certify that _____, who is personally known, this day appeared before me personally and do acknowledge that he/she did sign, seal, and deliver the foregoing instrument of his/her free will and accord, for the purpose therein named and expressed.

IN WITNESS WHEREOF, I have hereunto set my hand and official seal, this _____ day of _____, _____.

Signed _____,
Notary Public

My Commission Expires _____

Johnny May

ID Theft
Affadavit

If you are disputing fraudulent debts and accounts opened by an identity thief, the ID Theft Affidavit now simplifies the process. Instead of completing different forms, you can use the ID Theft Affidavit to alert companies where a new account was opened in your name. The company can then investigate the fraud and decide the outcome of your claim.

Here's a list of some of the companies and organizations that accept or endorse the ID Theft Affidavit.

- ACA International
- American Bankers Association
- America's Community Bankers
- AT&T
- Bank of America

- Call for Action
- Capital One
- Chase Manhattan Bank
- Computer Sciences Corporation
- Council of Better Business Bureaus
- Direct Marketing Association
- Equifax
- Experian
- Federal Reserve Board
- Fifth Third Bank
- First National Bank of Omaha
- Fleet Boston Financial
- GE Capital
- GetThere LP
- Identity Theft Resource Center
- Merrill Lynch
- Nissan Motor Acceptance Corporation
- Privacy Rights Clearinghouse
- Providian
- SBC Service
- Sears
- The California Office of Privacy Protection
- TransUnion
- VW Credit

ID Theft Affidavit

Victim Information

(1) My full legal name is

_____

(First)   (Middle)   (Last)   (Jr., Sr., III)

(2) (If different from above) When the events described in this affidavit took place, I was known as:

_____

(First)   (Middle)   (Last)   (Jr., Sr., III)

(3) My date of birth is _____
                               (day/month/year)

(4) My Social Security number is _____

(5) My driver's license or identification card state and number are _____

(6) My current address is

_____

City _____ State _____ Zip Code _____

(7)   I have lived at this address since

_____

(month/year)

(8)   (If different from above) When the events described in this affidavit took place, my address was

_____

City _____ State _____ Zip Code _____

(9)   I lived at the address in Item 8 from

_____until _____

(month/year)   (month/year)

(10) My daytime telephone number is

(_____) _____

My evening telephone number is

(_____) _____

How the Fraud Occurred

Check all that apply for items 11 – 17:

(11) ❑ I did not authorize anyone to use my name or personal information to seek the money, credit, loans, goods or services described in this report.

(12) ❑ I did not receive any benefit, money, goods or services as a result of the events described in this report.

(13) ❑ My identification documents (for example, credit cards; birth certificate; driver's license; social security card; etc.) were stolen lost on or about_____.

(day/month/year)

(14) ❑ To the best of my knowledge and belief, the following person(s) used my information (for example, my name, address, date of birth, existing account numbers, Social Security number, mother's maiden name, etc.) or identification documents to get money, credit, loans, goods or services without my knowledge or authorization:

_____

Name (if known)

_____

Name (if known)

_____

Address (if known)

_____

Address (if known)

_____

Phone number(s) (if known)

_____

Phone number(s) (if known)

_____

Additional information (if known)

_____

Additional information (if known)

(15) ❏ I do NOT know who used my information or identification documents to get money, credit, loans, goods or services without my knowledge or authorization.

(16) ❏ Additional comments: (For example, description of the fraud, which documents or information were used or how the identity thief gained access to your information.)

_____

_____

_____

_____

_____

_____

(Attach additional pages as necessary)

Victim's Law Enforcement Actions

(17) (check one) I ❑ am ❑ am not willing to assist in the prosecution of the person(s) who committed this fraud.

(18) (check one) I ❑ am ❑ am not authorizing the release of this information to law enforcement for the purpose of assisting them in the investigation and prosecution of the person(s) who committed this fraud.

(19) (check all that apply) I ❑ have ❑ have not reported the events described in this affidavit to the police or other law enforcement agency. The police ❑ did ❑ did not write a report.

In the event you have contacted the police or other law enforcement agency, please complete the following:

_____   _____
(Agency #1)   (Officer/Agency personnel
                                 taking report)

_____   _____
(Date of report)   (Report number, if any)

_____   _____
(Phone number)   (email address, if any)

_____   _____

(Agency #2)   Officer/Agency personnel
taking report)

_____   _____

(Date of report)   (Report number, if any)

_____   _____

(Phone number)   (email address, if any)

Documentation Checklist

Please indicate the supporting documentation you are able to provide to the companies you plan to notify. Attach copies (NOT originals) to the affidavit before sending it to the companies.

(20) ❏ A copy of a valid government-issued photo-identification card (for example, your driver's license, state-issued ID card or your passport). If you are under 16 and don't have a photo-ID, you may submit a copy of your birth certificate or a copy of your official school records showing your enrollment and place of residence.

(21) ❏ Proof of residency during the time the disputed bill occurred, the loan was made or the other event took place (for example, a rental/lease agreement in your name, a copy of a utility bill or a copy of an insurance bill).

(22) ❑ A copy of the report you filed with the police or sher-
     iff's department. If you are unable to obtain a report or
     report number from the police, please indicate that in Item
     19. Some companies only need the report number, not a
     copy of the report. You may want to check with each
     company.

Signature

I declare under penalty of perjury that the information I have provided in this affidavit is true and correct to the best of my knowledge.

_____   _____
(signature)   (date signed)

Knowingly submitting false information on this form could subject you to criminal prosecution for perjury.

_____
(Notary)

[Check with each company. Creditors sometimes require notarization. If they do not, please have one witness (non-relative) sign below that you completed and signed this affidavit.]

Witness:

_____   _____
(signature)   (printed name)

_____   _____
(date)   (telephone number)

Fraudulent Account Statement

Completing this Statement

- Make as many copies of this page as you need. Complete a separate page for each company you're notifying and only send it to that company. Include a copy of your signed affidavit.
- List only the account(s) you're disputing with the company receiving this form. See the example below.
- If a collection agency sent you a statement, letter or notice about the fraudulent account, attach a copy of that document (NOT the original).

I declare (*check all that apply*):

❏ As a result of the event(s) described in the ID Theft Affidavit, the following

❏ account(s) was/were opened at your company in my name without my knowledge,

❏ permission or authorization using my personal information or identifying documents:

Creditor Name & Address*	Account Number	Type of unauthorized credit/goods /services provided by creditor (if known)	Date Issued or Opened	Amount/ Value Provided[†]
Example: Example Nat'l Bank 22 Main St. Columbus, OH 22722	01234567-89	Auto loan	01/05/2000	$25,500.00

*The company that opened account or provided the goods or services
[†]The amount charged or the cost of the goods/services

❑ During the time of the accounts described above, I had the following account open with your company:

Billing name _____

Billing address _____

Account number _____

[Source: Federal Trade Commission, www.ftc.gov/idtheft]

Johnny May

Letter of Dispute:
Template

Date:

Your name
Your street address
Your city, state, zip code

Fraud Victim Assistance Division
Credit Bureau
Street address
City, state, zip code

Dear Sir or Madam,

I am writing to dispute the following information in my file. The items I dispute are circled on the attached copy of the report I received. The first discrepancy is (**Be as specific and detailed as you can. Tell them exactly what you are disputing and why**). I am requesting that these items be deleted to correct the errors in my credit report.

Enclosed are copies of the credit report with discrepancies circled. (**Provide all the documentation you can get your hands on.**) Please investigate these matters and delete the disputed items as soon as possible.

Sincerely,

Your name

Enclosures: (List copies you have enclosed)

Johnny May

Creditor Dispute Letter: Template

Date:

Your name
Street address
City, state, zip code

Creditor's title
Street address
City, state, zip code

Dear Sir or Madam,

I am writing to clear my name and false bad credit as I am a victim of identity theft. Someone in (**indicate State**) has used my Social Security number and name to illegally open an account. I have never had an account with (**creditor's name**). I am requesting that the fraudulent account be removed from my name and damages or losses be recovered from the identity thief.

Enclosed is (**tell them what enclosures you have**). Please investigate this matter and correct the damage done by the identity thief as soon as possible.

Sincerely,

Your name

Enclosures: (**List enclosures**)

Johnny May

State Identity Theft Statutes

N OTE: Many of these statutes may be reviewed online. Go to the website for your state government for further information. States marked with * do not currently have their law available online.

States

Alabama*. . . . 2001 Al. Pub. Act 312; 2001 A1. SB 144

Alaska . . . . Alaska Stat § 11.46.180

Arizona . . . . Ariz. Rev. Stat. § 13-2008

Arkansas*. . . . . Ark. Code Ann. § 5-37-227

California . . . . Cal. Penal Code §§ 530.5-530.7

Colorado . . . . Colo. Rev Stat. § 18-5-102

Colo. Rev Stat. § 18-5-113

Connecticut . . . . 1999 Gen. Stat. § 53(a)-129(a)

Delaware. . . . . Del. Code Ann. tit. 11, § 854

Florida . . . . Fla. Stat. Ann. § 817.568
Georgia . . . . . Ga. Code Ann. §§ 16-9-121, 16-9-127
Hawaii* . . . . Haw. Rev. Stat. § 708-810z
Idaho . . . . Idaho Code § 18-3126
Illinois . . . . 720 Ill. Comp. Stat. 5/16 G
Indiana . . . . Ind. Code Ann. § 35-43-5-4 (2000)
Iowa . . . . Iowa Code § 715A.8
Kansas . . . . Kan. Stat. Ann. § 21-4018
Kentucky . . . . Ky. Rev. Stat. Ann. § 514.160
Louisiana . . . . La. Rev. Stat. Ann. § 14:67.16
Maine . . . . Me. Rev. Stat. Ann. tit. 17-A, § 354-2A
Maryland . . . . Md. Code Ann. art. 27 § 231
Massachusetts . . . . . . Mass. Gen. Laws ch. 266, § 37E
Michigan* . . . . Mich. Comp. Laws § 750.285
Minnesota . . . . Minn. Stat. Ann. § 609.527
Mississippi . . . . Miss. Code Ann. § 97-19-85
Missouri . . . . Mo. Rev. Stat. § 570.223
Montana* . . . . . H.B. 331, 2001 Leg. (not yet codified)
Nevada . . . . Nev. Rev. State. § 205.463-465
New Hampshire . . . . . . N.H. Rev. Stat. Ann. § 638:26
New Jersey . . . . N.J. Stat. Ann. § 2C:21-17
New Mexico . . . . H.B. 317, 2001 Leg, 45th Sess.
North Carolina . . . . N.C. Gen. Stat. § 14-113.20
North Dakota . . . . N.D. Cent. Codes § 12.1-23
Ohio . . . . Ohio Rev. Code Ann. § 2913.49
Oklahoma . . . . Okla. Stat. tit. 21, § 1533.1
Oregon . . . . Or. Rev. Stat. § 165.800
Pennsylvania* . . . . 18 Pa. Cons. State § 4120
Rhode Island . . . . R.I. Gen. Laws § 11-49.1-1

South Carolina . . . . S.C. Code Ann. § 16-13-500, 501

South Dakota . . . . . S.D. Codified Laws § 22-30A-3.1.

Tennessee* . . . . Tenn. Code Ann. § 39-14-150

Texas . . . . Tex. Penal Code § 32.51

Utah. . . . . Utah Code Ann. § 76-6-1101-1104

Virginia . . . . Va. Code Ann. § 18.2-186.3

Washington . . . . Wash. Rev. Code § 9.35.020

West Virginia . . . . W. Va. Code § 61-3-54

Wisconsin. . . . . Wis. Stat. § 943.201

Wyoming*. . . . . Wyo. Stat. Ann. § 6-3-901

U.S. Territories

Guam*. . . . . 9 Guam Code Ann. § 46.80

U.S. Virgin Islands* . . . . 14 VI Code Ann. §§ 3003

Johnny May

Identity Theft and Assumption Deterrence Act

IDENTITY THEFT AND ASSUMPTION DETERRENCE ACT

As amended by Public Law 105-318, 112 Stat. 3007 (Oct. 30, 1998)

An Act

To amend chapter 47 of title 18, United States Code, relating to identity theft, and for other purposes. [NOTE: Oct. 30, 1998 – [H.R. 4151]

Be it enacted by the Senate and House of Representatives of the United States of America in Congress assembled, [NOTE: Identity Theft and Assumption Deterrence Act of 1998.]

Sec.

001. Short Title

002. Constitutional Authority to Enact this Legislation.

003. Identity Theft

004. Amendment of Federal Sentencing Guidelines for Offenses Under Section 1028

005. Centralized Complaint and Consumer Education Service for Victims of Identity Theft

006. Technical Amendments to Title 18, United States Code

007. Redaction of Ethics Reports Filed by Judicial Officers and Employees

§ 001. Short Title. [NOTE: 18 USC 1001 note.]

This Act may be cited as the "Identity Theft and Assumption Deterrence Act of 1998".

§ 002. Constitutional Authority to Enact this Legislation. [NOTE: 18 USC 1028 note.]

The constitutional authority upon which this Act rests is the power of Congress to regulate commerce with foreign nations and among the several States, and the authority to make all laws which shall be necessary and proper for carrying into execution the powers vested by the Constitution in the Government of the United States or in any department or officer thereof, as set forth in article I, section 8 of the United States Constitution.

§ 003. Identity Theft.

(a) Establishment of Offense.—Section 1028(a) of title 18, United States Code, is amended—

(1) in paragraph (5), by striking "or" at the end;

(2) in paragraph (6), by adding "or" at the end;

(3) in the flush matter following paragraph (6), by striking "or attempts to do so,"; and

(4) by inserting after paragraph (6) the following:

"(7) knowingly transfers or uses, without lawful authority, a means of identification of another person with the intent to commit, or to aid or abet, any unlawful activity that constitutes a violation of Federal law, or that constitutes a felony under any applicable State or local law;".

(b) Penalties.—Section 1028(b) of title 18, United States Code, is amended—

(1) in paragraph (1)—

(A) in subparagraph (B), by striking "or" at the end;

(B) in subparagraph (C), by adding "or" at the end; and

(C) by adding at the end the following:

"(D) an offense under paragraph (7) of such subsection that involves the transfer or use of 1 or more means of identification if, as a result of the offense, any individual committing the offense obtains anything of value aggregating $1,000 or more during any 1-year period;";

(2) in paragraph (2)–

(A) in subparagraph (A), by striking "or transfer of an identification document or" and inserting ", transfer, or use of a means of identification, an identification document, or a"; and

(B) in subparagraph (B), by inserting "or (7)" after "(3)";

(3) by amending paragraph (3) to read as follows:

"(3) a fine under this title or imprisonment for not more than 20 years, or both, if the offense is committed–

"(A) to facilitate a drug trafficking crime (as defined in section 929(a)(2));

"(B) in connection with a crime of violence (as defined in section 924(c)(3)); or

"(C) after a prior conviction under this section becomes final;";

(4) in paragraph (4), by striking "and" at the end;

(5) by redesignating paragraph (5) as paragraph (6); and

(6) by inserting after paragraph (4) the following:

"(5) in the case of any offense under subsection (a), forfeiture to the United States of any personal property used or intended to be used to commit the offense; and".

(c) Circumstances.—Section 1028(c) of title 18, United States Code, is amended by striking paragraph (3) and inserting the following:

"(3) either—

"(A) the production, transfer, possession, or use prohibited by this section is in or affects interstate or foreign commerce; or

"(B) the means of identification, identification document, false identification document, or document- making implement is transported in the mail in the course of the production, transfer, possession, or use prohibited by this section.".

(d) Definitions.—Subsection (d) of section 1028 of title 18, United States Code, is amended to read as follows:

"(d) In this section—

"(1) the term `document-making implement' means any implement, impression, electronic device, or computer hardware or software, that is specifically configured or primarily used for making an identification document, a false identification document, or another document-making implement;

"(2) the term `identification document' means a document made or issued by or under the authority of the United States Government, a State, political subdivision of a State, a foreign government, political subdivision of a foreign government, an international governmental or an international quasi-governmental organization which, when completed with information concerning a particular individual, is of a type intended or commonly accepted for the purpose of identification of individuals; "(3) the term 'means of identification' means any name or number that may be used, alone or in conjunction with any other information, to identify a specific individual, including any—

"(A) name, Social Security number, date of birth, official State or government issued driver's license or identification number, alien registration number, government passport number, employer or taxpayer identification number;
"(B) unique biometric data, such as fingerprint, voice print, retina or iris image, or other unique physical representation;
"(C) unique electronic identification number, address, or routing code; or
"(D) telecommunication identifying information or access device (as defined in section 1029(e));

"(4) the term 'personal identification card' means an identification document issued by a State or local government solely for the purpose of identification;

"(5) the term `produce' includes alter, authenticate, or assemble; and

"(6) the term `State' includes any State of the United States, the District of Columbia, the Commonwealth of Puerto Rico, and any other commonwealth, possession, or territory of the United States.".

(e) Attempt and Conspiracy.—Section 1028 of title 18, United States Code, is amended by adding at the end the following:

"(f) Attempt and Conspiracy.—Any person who attempts or conspires to commit any offense under this section shall be subject to the same penalties as those prescribed for the offense, the commission of which was the object of the attempt or conspiracy.".

(f) Forfeiture Procedures.—Section 1028 of title 18, United States Code, is amended by adding at the end the following:

"(g) Forfeiture Procedures.—The forfeiture of property under this section, including any seizure and disposition of the property and any related judicial or administrative proceeding, shall be governed by the provisions of section 413 (other than subsection (d) of that section) of the Comprehensive Drug Abuse Prevention and Control Act of 1970 (21 U.S.C. 853).".

(g) Rule of Construction.—Section 1028 of title 18, United States Code, is amended by adding at the end the following:

"(h) Rule of Construction.—For purpose of subsection (a)(7), a single identification document or false identification document that contains 1 or more means of identification shall be construed to be 1 means of identification.".

(h) Conforming Amendments.—Chapter 47 of title 18, United States Code, is amended—

(1) in the heading for section 1028, by adding "and information" at the end; and

(2) in the table of sections at the beginning of the chapter, in the item relating to section 1028, by adding "and information" at the end.

§ 004. Amendment of Federal Sentencing Guidelines for Offenses Under Section 1028. [NOTE: 28 USC 994 note.]

(a) In General.—Pursuant to its authority under section 994(p) of title 28, United States Code, the United States Sentencing Commission shall review and amend the Federal sentencing guidelines and the policy statements of the Commission, as appropriate, to provide an appropriate penalty for each offense under section 1028 of title 18, United States Code, as amended by this Act.

(b) Factors for Consideration.—In carrying out subsection (a), the United States Sentencing Commission shall consider, with respect to each offense described in subsection (a)—

(1) the extent to which the number of victims (as defined in section 3663A(a) of title 18, United States Code) involved

in the offense, including harm to reputation, inconvenience, and other difficulties resulting from the offense, is an adequate measure for establishing penalties under the Federal sentencing guidelines;

(2) the number of means of identification, identification documents, or false identification documents (as those terms are defined in section 1028(d) of title 18, United States Code, as amended by this Act) involved in the offense, is an adequate measure for establishing penalties under the Federal sentencing guidelines;

(3) the extent to which the value of the loss to any individual caused by the offense is an adequate measure for establishing penalties under the Federal sentencing guidelines;

(4) the range of conduct covered by the offense;

(5) the extent to which sentencing enhancements within the Federal sentencing guidelines and the court's authority to sentence above the applicable guideline range are adequate to ensure punishment at or near the maximum penalty for the most egregious conduct covered by the offense;

(6) the extent to which Federal sentencing guidelines sentences for the offense have been constrained by statutory maximum penalties;

(7) the extent to which Federal sentencing guidelines for the offense adequately achieve the purposes of sentencing set forth in section 3553(a)(2) of title 18, United States Code; and

(8) any other factor that the United States Sentencing Commission considers to be appropriate.

§ 005. Centralized Complaing and Consumer Education Service for Victims of Identity Theft. [NOTE: 18 USC 1028 note.]

(a) In <<NOTE: Deadline.>> General.–Not later than 1 year after the date of enactment of this Act, the Federal Trade Commission shall establish procedures to–

> (1) log and acknowledge the receipt of complaints by individuals who certify that they have a reasonable belief that 1 or more of their means of identification (as defined in section 1028 of title 18, United States Code, as amended by this Act) have been assumed, stolen, or otherwise unlawfully acquired in violation of section 1028 of title 18, United States Code, as amended by this Act;
> (2) provide informational materials to individuals described in paragraph (1); and
> (3) refer complaints described in paragraph (1) to appropriate entities, which may include referral to–

>> (A) the 3 major national consumer reporting agencies; and
>> (B) appropriate law enforcement agencies for potential law enforcement action.

(b) Authorization of Appropriations.–There are authorized to be appropriated such sums as may be necessary to carry out this section.

§ 006. Technical Amendments to Title 18, United States Code.

(a) Technical Correction Relating to Criminal Forfeiture Procedures.—Section 982(b)(1) of title 18, United States Code, is amended to read as follows: "(1) The forfeiture of property under this section, including any seizure and disposition of the property and any related judicial or administrative proceeding, shall be governed by the provisions of section 413 (other than subsection (d) of that section) of the Comprehensive Drug Abuse Prevention and Control Act of 1970 (21 U.S.C. 853).".

(b) Economic Espionage and Theft of Trade Secrets as Predicate Offenses for Wire Interception.—Section 2516(1)(a) of title 18, United States Code, is amended by inserting "chapter 90 (relating to protection of trade secrets)," after "to espionage),".

§ 007. Redaction of Ethics Reports Filed by Judicial Officers and Employees.

Section 105(b) of the Ethics in Government Act of 1978 (5 U.S.C. App.) is amended by adding at the end the following new paragraph:

"(3)(A) This section does not require the immediate and unconditional availability of reports filed by an individual described in section 109(8) or 109(10) of this Act if a finding is made by the Judicial Conference, in consultation with United States Marshall Service, that revealing personal and sensitive information could endanger that individual.

"(B) A report may be redacted pursuant to this paragraph only—

"(i) to the extent necessary to protect the individual who filed the report; and

"(ii) for as long as the danger to such individual exists.

"(C) The Administrative Office of the United States Courts shall submit to the Committees on the Judiciary of the House of Representatives and of the Senate an annual report with respect to the operation of this paragraph including—

"(i) the total number of reports redacted pursuant to this paragraph;

"(ii) the total number of individuals whose reports have been redacted pursuant to this paragraph; and

"(iii) the types of threats against individuals whose reports are redacted, if appropriate.

"(D) The Judicial Conference, in consultation with the Department of Justice, shall issue regulations setting forth the circumstances under which redaction is appropriate under this paragraph and the procedures for redaction.[NOTE: Regulations.]

"(E) This paragraph shall expire on December 31, 2001, and apply to filings through calendar year 2001.". [NOTE: Expiration date.]

Approved October 30, 1998.

LEGISLATIVE HISTORY—H.R. 4151 (S. 512):

SENATE REPORTS: No. 105-274 accompanying S. 512 (Comm. on the Judiciary).

CONGRESSIONAL RECORD, Vol. 144 (1998):

Oct. 7, considered and passed House.
Oct. 14, considered and passed Senate.

WEEKLY COMPILATION OF PRESIDENTIAL DOCUMENTS, Vol. 34 (1998):

Oct. 30, Presidential statement.

Johnny May

Personal Information Security Act

Source: American Legislative Exchange Council (ALEC)

Summary

This Act will define the criminal offense of identity theft or fraud and provide penalties for those convicted of the offense of identity theft or fraud. This Act also creates an identity theft bureau in the {insert state law enforcement agency} and an identity theft division in the office of the state attorney general to coordinate the investigation, apprehension, and prosecution of identity theft offenders and to provide a central clearing house for victims of identity theft to clear their personal records.

Model Bill

Section 1. This Act shall be cited as the "Personal Information Security Act."

Section 2. Definitions

A. "Personal identifying information" means any information designed, commonly used or capable of being used, alone or in conjunction with any other information, to identify a person, including, but not limited to: The name, address, telephone number, driver's license number, Social Security number, savings account number, checking account number, credit card number, debit card number, date of birth, place of employment and maiden name of the mother of a person.

B. "Document" includes, but is not limited to official documents containing personal identifying information, or a photocopy print, Photostat and other replica of an official document.

Section 3.

A. It is a violation of this act to use another's personal identifying information with fraudulent intent.

B. It is a violation of this act for a person to possess, sell or transfer any document or personal identifying information for fraudulent intent for himself or any other person.

Section 4. Penalties

A. A person who violates Section 3, subsection A. or B. is guilty of a crime of the {enter appropriate penalty and fine} if the pecuniary benefit, the value of the services received, the payment sought to be avoided or the injury or fraud perpetrated on another is $75,000 or more.

B. A person who violates Section 3, subsection A. or B. is guilty of a crime of the {enter appropriate lesser penalty and fine} if the pecuniary benefit, the value of the services received, the payment sought to be avoided or the injury or fraud perpetrated on another is at least $500 but is less than $75,000.

C. A person who violates Section 3, subsection A. or B. is guilty of a crime of the {enter appropriate lesser penalty and fine} if the pecuniary benefit the value of the services received, the payment sought to be avoided or the injury or fraud perpetrated on another is at least $100 but is less than $500.

D. If the pecuniary benefit, the value of the services received, the payment sought to be avoided or the injury or fraud perpetrated on another is less than $100, or if the benefit or services received or the injury or fraud perpetrated on another has no pecuniary value, or if the person was unsuccessful in an attempt to receive a benefit or services or to injure or perpetrate a fraud on another, then the person is guilty of a {low class misdemeanor}.

E. In a proceeding under this Act, the crime will be considered to have been committed in any locality where the person whose personal information was appropriated resides, or in which any part of the offense took place, regardless of whether the defendant was ever actually in that locality.

F. In addition to any other penalty, the court shall order a person convicted of violating Section 3, subsection A. or B. to pay restitution, including, without limitation, any attorney's fees and costs incurred to:

(a) Repair the credit history or rating of the person whose personal identifying information he obtained and used in violation of Section 3, subsection A. or B.; and

(b) Satisfy a debt, lien or other obligation incurred by the person whose personal identifying information he obtained and used in violation of Section 3, subsection A. or B.

Section 5. Creation of Identity Theft Bureau and Division

A. The identity theft bureau is created in the {insert name of state law enforcement agency}, to consist of law enforcement officers, assistant attorneys general, and representatives of county prosecuting attorneys experienced in the investigation, apprehension, and prosecution of identity theft offenders. The bureau shall coordinate and assist efforts of law enforcement agencies, prosecuting attorneys, and the attorney general in investigating, apprehending, and prosecuting offenders under this Act.

B. An identity theft division is created in the office of the state attorney general to assist citizens in the prevention, education, and prosecution of identity theft. The identity theft division shall:

(a) Provide a central point of consumer information and education on issues related to identity theft;

(b) Provide technical assistance to businesses developing policies regarding the use of nonpublic personal information, including developing model information privacy policies;

(c) Assist and coordinate with the identity theft bureau of the {insert name of state law enforcement agency} in the prosecution of crimes related to identity theft; and

(d) Serve as a state-wide clearinghouse to assist victims of identity theft in clearing their personal records in a timely manner.

Johnny May

Fraud Alert and Victim Statement Placement

The charts in this appendix describe the current fraud-alert and victim-statement placement procedures of the credit bureaus. *Fraud alerts* let creditors know that fraud has been associated with your credit report. As a result, creditors may confirm that they're dealing with you and not an imposter before granting credit or other services. *Victim statements* tell creditors to contact you before granting credit or other services. Victim statements may cause delays in getting credit while the creditor tries to contact you. If you have a cell phone, you may want to include that number in your statement. Please note that TransUnion and Equifax use a combined fraud alert and victim statement. Be sure to confirm these procedures when you contact the credit bureaus as they may change.

Initial Alert			
Credit Bureau	Period of Initial Coverage	Can You Request an Alert Online?	Is a Free Credit Report Provided?
TransUnion	12 months	No	Yes
Equifax	6 months	No	Yes
Experian	3 month fraud alert	No	Yes, can be provided online

Renewals			
CreditBureau	Period of Renewal Coverage	Is a Free Credit Report Provided?	Number of Renewals Allowed
TransUnion	12 months or 7 years	Yes	Unlimited
Equifax	6 months or 7 years	Yes	Unlimited
Experian	3 month fraud alert or 7 year victim statement	Yes, provided online	Unlimited

Johnny May

Endnotes

Chapter 1 • Identity Theft: An Overview

[1]Federal Trade Commission, FTC Releases Survey of Identity Theft in U.S. 27.3 Million Victims In Past 5 Years, Billions in Losses for Businesses and Consumers, http://www.ftc.gov/opa/2003/09/idtheft.htm.

[2]U.S. General Accounting Office, Identity Theft: Prevalence and Cost Appear to be Growing, March 2002.

[3]Ibid.

[4]"Calls Soar to FTC's Identity Theft Hotline," *APB-news.com*, July 12, 2000, http://www.apbnews.com/newscenter/breakingnews/ (site discontinued).

[5]Federal Trade Commission, Prepared statement of the Federal Trade Commission on Financial Identity Theft, April 22, 1999.

[6]Ibid.

[7]U.S. General Accounting Office, Identity Theft: Prevalence and Cost Appear to be Growing, March 2002.

[8]John Hanchette, "Identity Theft Tops List of Privacy Pirating," *Detroit News*, April 26, 2000.

[9]Anna Rau, "Enrollment Records Stolen from Local Grade School," *KTVB News*, http://ktvb.com/news/newstory.html?StoryID=11317.

[10]David Doege, "Scam Uses Names of Dead, Officials Say," *Milwaukee Journal Sentinel*, http://www.jsonline.com/news/metro/jun01/id0506040 01a.asp.

[11]Angela Atalla, "Seniors Targeted in Detroit Identity Theft," *Detroit Now*, http://www.detnow.com/news/0205281703.html.

[12]Consumer Reports Online, "Are You a Target for Identity Theft?" *Consumer Reports*, September 1997, http://www.consumerreports.com.

[13]A CALPIRG/Privacy Rights Clearinghouse Report, Nowhere to Turn: Victims Speak Out on Identity Theft, May 2000.

[14]Identity Theft Resource Center, Identity Theft: The Aftermath — 2003, September 23, 2003.

[15]"Identity Theft Model Bill Offered by Legislator Group," *U.S. Newswire*, October 4, 2001, http://www.usnewswire.com.

[16]Federal Trade Commission, Identity Theft Hotline, http://www.consumer.gov/idtheft.

Chapter 2 • Technology and the Information Age

[1]R.O'Harrow and L. Leyden, "Firm Got Almost $1.5 Million in Federal Aid to Build Drivers License Database," *The Dallas Morning News*, February 18, 1999.

[2]"Identity Thieves Plunder the Web," *APBnews.com*, May 10, 2000, www.apbnews.com (site discontinued).

[3]"Two Minutes and $14.95 for a Credit Report," *APBnews.com*, May 10, 2000, www.apbnews.com (site discontinued).

[4]Tom Arnold, Internet Identity Theft: A Tragedy for Victims, White Paper, June 2000.

[5]FBI Press Room, FBI Says Web "Spoofing" Scams Are a Growing Problem, www.fbi.gov, July 21, 2003.

[6]Bob Sullivan, "Look Alike E-Mail Scams on the Rise," *MSNBC*, July 21, 2003, http://www.msnbc.com/news/941872.asp?0cv=cb20&tcp1=1.

[7]Jacob H. Fries, "Worker Accused of Selling Colleagues ID's Online," *The New York Times*, March 2, 2002.

[8]Bob Sullivan, "Net Thieves Caught in Action: Fraud Investigator Sets Sting, Watches Thieves Swap Info," *MSNBC*, April 15, 2002, http://www.msnbc.com/news/739128.asp?0dm=T269T`.

[9]Bob Sullivan, "ID Thieves Mine for Gold on Jail Sites," *MSNBC*, May 12, 2002, http://www.msnbc.com/news/750428.asp.

Chapter 3 • How Identity Thieves Steal

[1]"For Postal Thieves, Your Mailbox is a Mother Lode of Crime: All Those Number You Entrust to The Postal Service are Easy Pickings for Information-Age Crooks," *Los Angeles Times*, May 31, 2000.

[2]John Q. Newman, *Identity Theft: The Cybercrime of the Millenium*, (Port Townsend, WA: Loompanics Unlimited, 1999), 39.

[3]Louis R. Mizell Jr., *Invasion of Privacy*, (New York: Berkley Publishing Group, 1998), 77.

[4]"Hospital Security Tightened after Vets Hit by Scam," *Evansville Courier & Press*, August 20, 2001.

[5]"Dumpster Diving and Trashed Credit," *Los Angeles Times*, February 1, 1999.

[6]Susan Risdon, "Theft Ring Has Nearly a Dozen Cities on Alert," *MSNBC*, February 14, 2002, http://www.msnbc.com/local/kxas/NBC518B2NXC.asp.

[7]Better Business Bureau, Who's Swiping Your Credit Card, http://www.bbb.org/library/creditswip.asp.

[8]Protecting Your Plastic, *Dateline NBC*, NBC, November 29, 1999.

⁹Federal Trade Commission, Y2K Care: Protecting Your Finances from Year 2000 Scam Artists, Consumer Alert, March 1999.

¹⁰Federal Trade Commission, Prepared Statement of the Federal Trade Commission on Financial Identity Theft, April 22, 1999.

Chapter 4 • Prevention Strategies

¹Beth Schuster, "Gore Seeks Tougher Law Against Theft of Identity," *Los Angeles Times*, June 8, 2000.

²Cp l. Albert Jeffcoat, Coastal Empire Alliance Against Fraud, telephone interview, February 13, 2001.

³Traveler's Insurance CompanyTraveler's Property Casualty Provides Consumers First Insurance Protection Against Identity Theft Expenses, http://www.travelers.com/idfraud.html.

⁴Georgia Stop Identity Theft Network, What Georgia Is Doing to Stop Identity Theft, http://www.stopidentitytheft.org/press/pr_1html.

⁵CNN, "Visa Moves to Prevent Identity Theft," *CNN.com*, March 6, 2003, http://money.cnn.com/2003/03/06/news/companies/visa.reut.

Chapter 5 • Your Social Security Number

[1]Social Security Administration, Social Security: Your Number, Febraury 1998, http://www.ssa.gov.

[2]Chicago Sun Times News Service, *Omaha World - Telegram*, November 18 1981, pg. 34.

[3]"Social Insecurity," *MSNBC*, http://www.msnbc.com/news/431520.asp.

[4]Beth Givens, *The Privacy Rights Handbook*, (New York: Avon Books, 1997), 239.

Chapter 6 • False Identification

[1]Luke Reiter, Are You an Identity Theft Victim? TechTV, January 10, 2000.

[2]"2 Charged with $500,000 Fake-ID Fraud," *Orlando Sentinel*, August 17, 2001.

[3]"Alleged Theft Ring Stole More than 100 Identities," *Seattle Post-Intelligencer*, June 20, 2001.

[4]"Salem Woman Charged With Making Fake IDs," Associated Press, October 9, 2001.

[5]John Bellah, "Fraudulent Identification Documents," *Law & Order,* February 2001

[6]Michigan State Police, "Identifying Fraudulent and Fake Drivers Licenses," *The Tuebor*, Summer 2003.

[7]CNN, The Hidden Information in Your Driver's License, *CNN.com* September 8, 2002, http://www.cnn.com/2002/tech/ptech/09/08/id.scanners/index.html.

[8]"Internet Key to Do-It-Yourself Fake IDs," *USA Today*, July 2, 2001.

[9]Ibid.

Chapter 7 • If You Become a Victim

[1]Federal Trade Commission, Recovering From Identity Theft, www.consumer.gov.idtheft/.

[2]Federal Trade Commission, Press Release: Federal Trade Commission Announces ID Theft Affidavit, February 5, 2002.

[3]FDIC Consumer News, A Crook Has Drained Your Account. Who Pays? Spring 1998, http://www.fdic.gov/consumers/news/cnsprg98/crook.html.

[4]Linda Goldman-Foley, Identity Theft: Organizing Your Case, Fact Sheet #17b, http://www.privacyrights.org.

Chapter 8 • Identity Theft in the Workplace

[1]"Ring of Identity Thieves Busted," *USA Today*, November 26, 2002.

[2]"General Motors Executives Victims of Credit Card Fraud," *Detroit Free Press*, February 11, 2000.

[3]"Employee Accused of Identity Theft, *Associated Press*, March 5, 2002.

[4]TransUnion, Criminal Intent: Top Underlying Causes of Credit Fraud and Identity Theft, http://www.transunion.com.

[5]"Employment Records Prove Ripe Source for Identity Theft," *USA Today* January 23, 2003.

[6]WISN 12 News, Bank Customers Information Sold to Identity Theft Ring, broadcast, May 22, 2002.

[7]Susan J. Wells "Stolen Identity," *HR Magazine*, vol 47, no.12, December 2002.

[8]AHI's Employment Resource Center, Identity Theft Invades the Workplace, March 4, 2003, http://www.ahipubs.com.

[9]Fox 23 News, New Type of Identity Theft Targets Business Information Collection, broadcast, April 14, 2003.

[10]"New Law Takes Aim at ID Theft," *San Francisco Chronicle*, June 11, 2002.

[11]Used PC's May Leak Sensitive Secrets, ZD Net, August 20, 2001, http://www.zdnet.com.

Chapter 9 • Identity Theft Case Files

[1]John Ingold, "Thanks to Thieves, Checks No Longer in the Mail," *Denver Post*, December 20, 2000.

[2]*The Edmonton Sun*, "Credit Card Scam at Vancouver Airport: Rip-off Operated from Improvement Booth," November 19, 2000.

[3]Francine Latour, "Arrest Disrupts False ID, Title Ring Allegedly Used Registry Records," *The Boston Globe*, December 13, 2000.

4"FTC Chief Fell Prey to Credit Card Fraud," *APB-news.com*, March 16, 2000, http://www.apbnews.com (site discontinued).

5Margaret Mannix, "Stolen Identity Can Ruin Your Credit – and That's Not the End," *U.S. News*, June 1, 1998, http://www.usnews.com/usnews/issue/980601/1Thef.htm.

6PIRG report, "Theft of Identity: The Consumer X-files," August 1996, 6-7.

7Mark Larabee, "Identity Crime Fought Face-To-Face: Law Enforcement Agencies Joining Forces Against Rising C," *The Oregonian*, September 21, 2000.

8Jan Faust, "Dealing with Identity Theft," *ABC-news.com*, October 9, 1998, http://abcnews.go.com/sections/us/DailyNews/id_theft981006.html.

9Timothy O'Brien, "Identity Theft is Crime of Digital Era, Thanks to Net," *Seattle-PI.com*, http://seattlepi.nwsource.com/national/iden03.shtml.

10Rick Sarlat, "Police: Woman Stole ID to Pay for Childbirth," *APBnews.com*, November 2, 2000, http://www.apbnews.com/newscenter/breakingnews/200/11/02/insurance1102_01.html (site discontinued).

[11]M.L. Elrick, "13 Charged in Theft of Seniors' Names," *Detroit Free Press*, October 17, 2000.

[12]Todd Venezia, "Police: Woman had 350 Stolen Identities," *APBnews.com*, March 24, 2000, http://www.apbnews.com/newscenter/breakingnews/2000/03/24/spytheft0324_01.h (site discontinued).

[13]L.A. Johnson, "The Victim Had a Name to Die For," *Detroit Free Press*, May 13, 1994.

[14]Frances Ann Burns, "Worker Accused of Stealing Cancer Patient Info," *APBnews.com*, August 8, 2000, http://www.apbnews.com/newscenter/breakingnews/2000/08/08/patientsc808_.htm (site discontinued).

[15]"Tiger Woods a Victim of Identity Theft," *APBnews.com*, December 19, 2000, http://www.apb.com/newscenter/breakingnews/.../tiger1219_01htm (site discontinued).

[16]"Morgue Workers Accused of Stealing From dead," *APBnews.com*, December 20, 2000, http://www.apb.com/newscenter/breakingnews/morgue1220_01.htm (site discontinued).

[17]Mia Tran, "ID Thieves Muscle in on Cars at Fitness Clubs," *Los Angeles Times*, June 4, 2002.

[18]Larry Neumeister, "Man Sentenced for Credit Card Fraud," *Associated Press*, May 28, 2002.

[19]Jackie Hallifax, "Inmate Accused of Identity Theft Ring," *Associated Press*, July 25, 2001.

[20]KCRA, "Children taken Away from Identity Theft Victim," *TheKCRAChannel.com*, April 23, 2002, http://www.TheKCRAChannel.com/.

[21]Larry Savino, "VA Employees Accused of bringing Dead Vets Back to Life to Steal Benefits," *Knight Ridder*, August 30, 2001.

[22]Betsy Blaney, "Man Pleads Guilty to Using Three Stooges Firm in Fraud Scheme," *San Francisco Gate*, August 28, 2001.

Johnny May

Index

D

Database, 17, 33, 65, 76
Deceased, 4-5, 89
Department of Justice, 11, 101
Department of Motor Vehicles
(DMV), 59, 84
Digital photos, 13
Drivers License, 4, 13, 34, 40,
57, 59-60, 71, 89, 152
Dumpster Diving, 23

E

E-mail, 16, 42, 76, 98-99
Electronic Bulletin Boards, 17
Electronics Funds Transfer
Act, 67
Employees, 38, 44-45, 59, 77-
78, 80, 84, 91
Employer Liability, 78
Employers, 43, 49, 54, 77
Equifax, 36, 39, 64, 94-95,
112, 157-158
Experian, 36, 39, 64, 94-95,
112, 158

F

Fair Credit Billing Act, 68
Fair Credit Reporting Act, 68
False Identification, 19, 57-61
FBI, 11, 16, 86, 91
Federal Trade Commission, 1,
77, 85, 97, 101
Feinstein, Diane, 51
Firewalls, 42, 46
Fraud, 0-2, 16-17, 32, 39, 52-
53, 64, 66-67, 69, 71-72,
77, 90, 93-94, 101-102,
107, 111, 151, 153, 157-
158

Fraud Alert, 64, 66-67, 157-
158
Fraudulent Address Change, 23
Freedom of Information Act,
16

G

Genealogy, 18, 27, 40
General Accounting Office, 3
Georgia Stop Identity Theft
Network, 32-33

H

Hacking, 15

I

ID Theft Affidavit, 65, 111
Identity Theft and
Assumption Deterrence
Act, 11, 135, 137-149
Identity Theft Resource
Center, 9, 99, 101, 112
Information Brokers, 18, 51
Insider Access, 26
Internet, 0, 13-18, 27, 40, 50,
60, 76, 79, 87
Internet Service Provider
(ISP), 15-16
IRS, 53-54, 71

L

Laws, 10, 68, 79, 134-135
Lawsuits, 5
Lexis-Nexis, 50
Liability, 67-68, 78
Los Angeles County Sheriff's
Department, 31

About the Author

Johnny May, a widely respected and highly sought after security professional, is an independent security consultant and trainer specializing in protecting individuals and organizations from identity theft.

He has lectured extensively on security and crime prevention topics, and he is regularly cited by the media as a leading authority on identity theft prevention. He has appeared on NBC Nightly News with Tom Brokaw, A&E Open Book, Comcast Newsmakers, and numerous other television and radio talk shows. He has also been featured in publications such as Consumers Digest, Entrepreneur, and The Robb Report.

Mr. May is a graduate of the University of Detroit-Mercy, where he earned his B.S. in Criminal Justice and his M.S. in Security Administration. He is an adjunct professor at the University of Detroit-Mercy, Madonna University, and Henry Ford Community College.

Johnny May has been designated as a Certified Protection Professional (CPP) by ASIS International, and he is board certified in security management.

For seminar information contact Johnny May at:

P.O. Box 7754, Bloomfield Hills, MI 48302
www.identitytheftinfo.com • secres@prodigy.net

Johnny May